Mission
to Soho

WHERE TWO WORLDS MEET

© Day One Publications 2020

ISBN 978-1-84625-671-4

British Library Cataloguing in Publication Data available

Published by Day One Publications
Ryelands Road, Leominster, HR6 8NZ
Telephone 01568 613 740
North America Toll Free 888 329 6630
email—sales@dayone.co.uk
web site—www.dayone.co.uk

The images on the cover are used under licence from Shutterstock.com

Printed by 4edge Limited

Contents

Contents

Foreword

H ere is the story of what it means to live among a community that is despised and considered of little real value, often in a squalid and deprived environment. Michael and Pam Toogood shared their lives with this community in the deepest possible way. They were pioneers in the truest sense, and they have much to teach us from their successes and mistakes. It is an honest and robust account of what it takes to be a cross-cultural missionary in the most degraded yet colourful area of a great city. For any who admire the commitment of those who give up so much to take the gospel and live among a strange and often 'offensive' culture, this account will illustrate that the experience can be replicated in any of our great cities.

This city is London and the culture is Soho.

Written by a man of humility, who is constantly self-critical and makes light of his incredible energy, commitment and determination, this account of church planting in the toughest part of London is both humbling and deeply challenging. It is far more than simply a good read. It is the story of urban church planting with its raw and realistic challenges at a time when establishing new churches was in its infancy. Michael admits, 'I can't imagine church planting ever being done in this way again!' He is right. Back then in the 1980s the idea of a strong start-up team was little understood.

The story is written with a compelling use of words in the vivid descriptions of people and situations; it will often add a smile on your face or bring tears to your eyes. The Toogood family demonstrated a total commitment to the people they came to save through serving. For them, people mattered as people and not simply as potential converts. Michael realised that 'Doing good for its own sake does not always fit our agenda of evangelism.'

His memories reveal how trusted and appreciated he and Pam were. The many cameos of people in their 'parish' are valuable insights into the deep level of care demanded if we are to reach the world in our neighbourhood. In order to establish a true local church, in a city where the largest churches imported much of their congregation each Sunday, the Christians of Immanuel Church Soho did not commute into the area once a week—they lived there. An indispensable lesson for any church planting or revitalising.

Read with discernment and humility there is much here for all churches to learn, especially a preparedness to live alongside the ugly squalor of deprivation, drug and alcohol abuse and more. It also reveals a passion to seize any and every opportunity for the gospel, however much 'nice' Christians might criticise. Michael and Pam did what Jesus did—and it was costly.

The true quality of Michael Toogood as a committed Christian, pastor and evangelist, is revealed in the fact that he has shown no let-up in service for the gospel in retirement, bereavement and personal ill-health. It is not possible to read this account and remain comfortable and complacent with our own meagre commitment to Christ.

Brian H Edwards
January 2020

Preparation for planting

T he envelope looked suspicious from the moment it landed on my desk. It was brown, DL size, with a handwritten address. I thought I recognized the handwriting.

Pam and I were in the seventh year of serving the church in the London over-spill town of Thamesmead. Begun in the 1960s, the new town was still in the process of being built. Eventually there would be fifty thousand homes, grouped into ten distinct areas. Our church was serving Area 3, which consisted of around two thousand homes. It had its own shopping precinct, community centre, pub, medical centre and two junior schools. For many residents, it was a great improvement on their previous inner London two-up, two-down, back-to-back homes. Whole families were settled here; it was even possible to bring your elderly parents with you.

In 1975 we had been invited by sixty London Grace Baptist churches to lead a team to establish a new church in Area 3. This would uproot us from the flourishing New Cross church we had served for the previous ten years. The local authority would provide temporary accommodation for us until the church complex was completed in eighteen months' time. The home, in Malthus Path, was a town house, built over three levels. We found ourselves living among a few early arrivals who had been uprooted from a variety of south-east London boroughs and re-homed among the mud and concrete of this new town by the Thames. It was good to arrive before the bulk of our neighbours, so that we could welcome them as fellow residents.

A team would join us later, but the initial groundwork was down to us: Pam making contact with the schools, local mums and immediate neighbours, while I built bridges with the Development Team, social workers, and families already living here through door-to-door visiting.

The reward of living in Thamesmead was the icy wind that blew unhindered from the bleak wastelands of the Essex coast on the other side of the Thames.

The progress of the work was surprising, given where we were. We outgrew our home as a base for meetings, and secured the use of the local community club-room for a Sunday morning service. The smell of stale beer and smoke from the previous evening may not have been conducive to worship, but we soon became a congregation in double figures. There was pressure to finish on time each Sunday, because the club-room bar opened promptly at noon!

There were signs the Lord was working as we worked. Our immediate neighbour, a tough ex-army Christian from Northern Ireland, who had been provided accommodation because of his involvement in the troubles of that time, re-committed himself to the Lord, and to us. His wife with another young mother and our eldest son were converted during the eighteen months we worshipped and learned together in that dank, smelly room. It was also possible to begin a midweek meeting for prayer and Bible study in a cramped ground floor room in our home.

When we moved into the new church complex in mid-1977, the Sunday congregation rapidly grew to thirty-five. Midweek youth work flourished, and a waiting list was necessary. Good contact with a local Scout group resulted in a monthly Parade Service, with one hundred and thirty people of all ages attending.

Eventually, the team came together as we hoped. Bill and Sue Lyall, having completed their training with a church in Greenwich, came to serve with us full-time. Mary O'Neil arrived soon after, completing the team. Her nursing background proved to be an asset among the many local young mothers. The entire team was accommodated within Area 3, and that was a major bonus.

Normal life in an urban sprawl

A few not untypical events that occurred during our seven and a half years in Thamesmead illustrate the life of a church planter in an urban setting and, although we didn't realise it, they were a preparation for what was to come.

In the early hours of one Sunday morning, we were woken by an urgent ringing on the front door. A young woman stood on the step—bleeding from knife wounds inflicted by her violent boyfriend.

Over several years, a lecturer brought a class of trainee teachers from South Wales for a day to expose them to all aspects of life in a 1970s new town and the church which served it. Another team of young people came for a week of outreach to help us with our visiting, literature distribution and youth work. For two days we introduced them to the area and the work we were doing before letting them loose under the guidance of their young leader. They were climbing the steps of a five-story block of flats when the body of a young man plunged to the ground—his girlfriend having rejected him. The totally distressed team headed home early the following morning.

A young mother popped into the local supermarket for emergency shopping, leaving her three year-old son in his buggy, outside. It was only for a minute or two but the three year-old was fascinated by the canal a few feet away. Somehow, he slipped out of his harness, made his way down the steps, tripped and fell into the deep water. No-one was there to raise the alarm and the child was drowned. His distraught parents called me. I took the grieving father to identify the body in the mortuary, where he collapsed. Later, I agreed to have the small coffin in the church overnight, and to conduct a simple service the following day before taking the committal in a nearby cemetery. I will never forget the mother's anguished cries.

In the early days, most of the 'professionals' working in Area 3 got to know each other and were often in touch, sharing issues and people in need. A call from a school secretary one lunch time shared her concern that a mother had called into the office, her face showing signs of having been beaten: 'Would I call and check if she needed help?' Wondering if I would end up with wounds of my own if the husband was at home, I knocked on the door. I was invited in. There was no husband around. It was true, her husband had lashed out having had too much to drink. It had happened before. No, she didn't need medical care, or want the police to get involved—she reckoned this was part of normal family life She had grown up with violence in her parents' home—it's what happens in families isn't it?

I'll never forget the father and two little girls who called at our home with toys for refugee children at Christmas time. The father was an alcoholic, and the young mother was dying of cancer. I visited the home the next day. 'Will you take care of my girls?' the fragile mother asked. I promised to do all I could. She died two weeks later. I regularly visited the father, who was usually the worse for drink. Every evening, at 11 pm, I walked our dog past the family home to check the girls were in bed. If they were still up I took them home, where Pam had a bed prepared for them. Eventually, the girls were taken into care while they were at school. We were asked to be there to smooth the way. I explained that they could call me, or ask me to visit, at any time. Some months later there was a farewell party before the girls travelled to Australia, to live with their mother's sister. I heard nothing of them for thirty-seven years until the eldest girl, now in her 40s and married with two children, traced me by email to say, 'Thank you' and to ask me to fill in the gaps of her early childhood. Her younger sister is also regularly in touch, sharing the athletic successes, and ailments, of her two sporty children.

Lessons in preparation

We learned many lessons as church planters in a deprived urban setting—often by making mistakes!

There is no doubt of the value of church planters living among the people they are seeking to reach with the gospel. Help of all kinds is often a long way away in emergency situations in newly developed areas, but Christians right there can help in critical situations.

There can be no substitute for a servant heart—being ready at all hours of the day and night, whatever the need. A prayer meeting was interrupted by the frantic cries of an elderly neighbour. Her husband had jacked his ailing car onto bricks so that he could crawl underneath for the repair. The bricks gave way and the man was crushed. Tragically, he didn't survive—but we were there to do what was necessary at the time, and after.

There can be no substitute for a servant heart—being ready at all hours of the day and night, whatever the need

Maintaining immediate and daily contact with the community to build relationships is not possible at a distance. It was so helpful to be established within the community before the bulk of the families moved in. We were involved helping to carry in the furniture, and even laying the carpet. Several hours later we could be drinking tea in the kitchen, with a friendship made, and a witness demonstrated.

We saw the importance of maintaining a good working relationship with others heading up activity in the community. After all, they will go home at the end of the working day, while the church workers will be available throughout the day, night—and weekend. A phone call interrupted our Sunday lunch. Albert lived in a flat behind our home, needing time and support on a regular basis. 'I need to see you—now' he insisted down the phone. Pam put my meal in the oven. Invited into the flat, it was clear Albert was in a bad way. His fun-loving wife had told him she was off to London, and promptly left, leaving Albert dejected and rejected. 'Do you know,' he admitted, 'if you hadn't come when I called, I would have swallowed all of these!' pointing to the contents of several bottles of antidepressants scattered all over the coffee table. I had responded to Albert's call, so Albert lived, to be depressed again another day. My Sunday lunch ended up in the dog!

Consistency of living as a Christian in every area of life was clearly noticed because we lived among the people we were trying to reach for Jesus. The church building was set against a semicircle of some five hundred flats. Our lives were constantly on show. One team member was encouraging a resident to join us on Sunday, and although the invitation was declined she commented that she appreciated the way the minister came out of the manse when his wife arrived home with the family shopping, opened the car door for her, and the boot, and carried the heavy bags into the home. Apparently, that rarely happened on this estate and it was noticed!

Doing good for its own sake does not always fit our agenda of evangelism. Our immediate neighbours were a family of five—middle aged parents, and three grown up sons. The husband

> Doing good for its own sake does not always fit our agenda of evangelism

was confined to the home with a serious heart problem. A reclusive family, it wasn't easy to get close to them. Since the church buildings were surrounded by grassed areas we needed to invest in a lawn mower. A bargain was on offer in a nursery near Gravesend, Kent. I asked my neighbours if they would like to join me for the drive? They would—and it was a lovely outing, with refreshments en route! While easing the husband out of the car, the wife asked, 'Can anyone come to your church?' 'Oh, yes,' I said, 'It's for people just like me and you!' I was always welcomed into the home following the trip, and the woman rarely missed the morning service! I conducted the funerals of both parents in the coming years.

The brown envelope

Our aim at Thamesmead was to put ourselves out of work whenever possible, stepping aside to make room for leaders growing up within the ranks of the church membership. Members of the original team had moved to other work by early 1982, while Pam and I were wondering about our own future; we felt that in principle we too should move on, giving the church the freedom to call a man of its own choice. The church members had already recognized the leadership gifts of three men within the membership. However, the church still needed a full-time minister. Was I that man for the longer term?

It was while we were in the process of discovering God's will for the church and ourselves that the letter in the brown envelope, with the recognizable handwriting, arrived on my desk. It set out a new challenge. As I feared, Pam's response wasn't exactly: 'Praise the Lord, when do we start?' but she certainly had a gradual recognition that the Lord was behind this invitation. She was aware that I had been involved with a group of men who, for two years, walked the streets of Soho, one of the seediest and neediest areas in the heart of London, to discern if God wanted a gospel work there.

No doubt Pam had picked up on the enthusiasm I brought home when the conclusion was reached that there was a work to be done. 'That's one place I'm not going,' she said over breakfast, presuming that we had done our bit in moving to Thamesmead, and that someone else should step up this time.

Talking it over during the next few days, Pam clearly sensed that she would soon be uprooting once again. We moved first when I resigned from the Design Centre in 1962 to take up ministry with the Bexleyheath church; again in 1966 when we moved to the New Cross church; and ten years later to church plant in Thamesmead. Each move was challenging to Pam who would prefer a settled life as a mother to four children, home maker, active church member, and pastor's wife. The quality of the homes and areas in which we had lived and served over the past twenty years were never an issue, it was the upheaval for the children, their schooling, friendships and safety which were her chief concerns. Now the latest call to uproot demanded a move to a very different area.

Welcome to Soho

We left Thamesmead in July 1982. By now our two eldest children, Nick and Jo, were married and living away from home, leaving Lois a student, and Jon at a Lewisham prep school. Our accommodation needs would hopefully be sorted later, but a central London flat would inevitably mean culling our furniture, originally bought piece by piece, and virtually everything else we owned. When the time eventually came to move, almost all our furniture was carried away on barrows by local families in need, leaving us with just the bare essentials.

Great efforts were being made on our behalf to persuade Westminster Council to accommodate us in Soho—an almost impossible task, humanly speaking, given the demand for housing in every part of London. But the Lord was working for us. It was late August, and I was at a conference when the phone call came. A set of keys to a basement flat in the City of Westminster Dwellings in Marshall Street, just round the corner from Carnaby Street, could be collected. We had two hours to view, and to make up our minds if we wanted it or not before returning the keys. It was a take-it-or-leave-it deal. There was no alternative on offer.

Since this was to be our family home, all four of us went to the viewing. Marshall Street was easy to find, with a film studio on one side and the famous Marshall Street Baths on the other. When approaching the Victorian block of flats in the corner, I remembered that during our fact-finding mission some months before, I had felt strongly that this would be the ideal place for the team leader to live.

The main front door had a handle, but no lock. We went in, and down a dozen concrete steps to the four basement flats. We were in deep shadow. The smell of urine—and worse—was there to greet us. Number 4 was to our right. The door opened easily with a turn of the key, and the stench was eager to rush out and greet us; it left us gasping for breath, a foretaste of what we would find inside. There was a toilet without a door, and a kitchen just wide enough for one person to walk to the sink, turn round, and come out again; a cold water tap came out of the wall.

A living room lay ahead of us, ten feet square, minus the chimney breast; two windows faced Marshall Street, eight feet above us, from which we could see the legs of people passing by but no sky; a bare bulb hung down from the ceiling. Turning round to take in all the room had to offer, we noticed blood that must have spurted up the wall from an artery wound in some violent struggle.

A door led through to the main bedroom, just big enough to take an ordinary-sized double bed, while touching the wall on one side and at the head and foot. The second room was a box room, six feet by eleven, less the chimney breast. Water was running down the far wall. Nineteen year-old Lois, and twelve year-old Jon were going to have to share this space. Perhaps it would double up as a study area when free.

The stench was everywhere. But where was the bathroom? There wasn't one! Our personal washing would need to take place in the kitchen sink. Where was the heating system? There wasn't one, only a dilapidated gas fire.

The clock was ticking.

Clearly, the family dog would have to be re-homed, and Jon's cycle either left with friends or sold on. Could we face life here as a family? It was time for me to take the lead. I decided we could! This is what the Lord has provided for us and we must accept this home as his gracious provision. This was not the decision of some super-spiritual saint. Simply that I sensed the Lord in his wisdom would have us be here—and for his glory. We would have to trust him through the many areas of tension that we were bound to face.

Cleaning up and moving in

Westminster Council worked quickly. A Tenancy Agreement was drawn up, signed, returned, and the keys handed over. Now we had to make the flat hygienic and a comfortable space for family living. The flat was at least empty apart from layers of rotting cardboard which covered the living room floor. It seemed to us that this was largely responsible for the putrid smell. Pam and I arrived with buckets, disinfectant and elbow grease to deal with it as the first priority. On hands and knees we began stripping away the evil layers with our nails, encountering things which slithered and crawled, obviously unhappy about being disturbed. We filled buckets with the stinking stuff, dumping it in a waste bin in the street outside.

Pam and I had begun the work 10am, commenting on this and that, at least occasionally, but conversation soon dried up altogether as the stench filled our nostrils, and the slime got under our nails. Two hours had passed, when Pam suddenly stood up, saying she couldn't stand it for another moment. She went into the kitchen, washed her hands under the cold water tap, dried them on a cloth, put on her coat, picked up her bag, and walked out of the flat. My heart sank! We were just two hours into the project, and we had thrown in the towel already. I also rinsed my hands, shook them dry, and grabbed a coat just in time to see Pam heading for Soho Square. We sat silently on a vacant seat, Pam producing sandwiches and coffee from her bag. We ate and drank without saying a word. There are times when it is unwise to risk saying anything. Then, typical of the woman I had married twenty-five years before, Pam suddenly announced, 'Come on, let's get on with it!' We did and were rewarded with a beautifully preserved herring-bone wood block floor underneath the rubbish. There was a sermon on sanctification here somewhere.

Later that evening, back in the luxury of the Thamesmead manse, we agreed a practical solution to all that had to be done. Pam and I would divide our time and energies. I would travel to Soho from Monday to Saturday each week, strip out the flat completely, then repaint, decorate and carpet each room, while Pam would begin disposing of the furniture and everything that would not fit into the available space, and packing in boxes the things that would. My books would be stacked in cardboard boxes and left in Thamesmead, taking only the essentials that would fit a four foot long window ledge.

The scheme worked well. Pam was practical, systematically working through the large home and its contents. I travelled from Abbey Wood station at 7am each morning, worked for twelve hours, before returning

Our own toilet, though it had no door or handbasin

after the rush-hour in the evening, tired but pleased that the flat was progressing.

I occasionally met our new neighbours coming in and out of the building. Several of them were keen to check out who would be joining them in the Dwellings. One of them, a single man, invited me in for a cup of tea. He told stories of war-time heroics with the RAF, and

The second of two bedrooms when we moved in. Jon and Lois shared this 11 ft by 7 ft room which doubled as my study when unoccupied

delighted in the name of 'Duckworth,' with its historic aero connections. Years later my successor learned that the story was more than a little short on truth: he was plain John Smith, with no war-time heroics whatever. A taste of what was to come.

The flat was completed in six weeks. It looked good and smelt a great deal better. Illustrating its shoe-box size, the living room carpet from the Thamesmead home covered every area from the front door to the living room and both bedrooms, with enough left over to donate to a hard-pressed neighbour.

After six weeks of hard work, our 10 ft by 10 ft living area was ready. We could seat six people on folding chairs, if no one moved

We moved in during the evening of Friday, 8 October, Jon's twelfth birthday. It was raining and a sympathetic friend loaded our essential furniture and boxes on to a trailer and helped us pile them up in the living room. He didn't stay around too long.

It was getting late, therefore setting up the beds was a priority. Jon had a bunk bed above a desk unit, while Lois made do with a mattress on a sheet of plywood, fitted to the top of a timber frame, built in the chimney recess. It was the best we could do. Pam and I set about screwing the legs on to our double bed. Not having the space to walk round it, it was a work of art to set the bed down on the floor, and get the bed clothes tucked in. We were more than ready for our first night's sleep.

It was then we discovered something which was going to dominate our going to bed for the next few years: there wasn't space for both of us to undress at the same time. One of us had to go first, get into bed, leaving space for the other. Since there was no room to walk round the bed, the person sleeping next to the wall would either have to get in first or clamber over the one sleeping next to the door—which was Pam because she felt claustrophobic on the inside. We turned out the light and got under the covers. It was cold. Almost immediately, there was a creaking sound and the legs on my side of the bed gave way, sending us rolling across the mattress and piling up against the wall. We could only laugh, or we would have cried with frustration. Pulling the bed onto its side (with difficulty) the legs were screwed on more securely. With the bedding arranged, it was eventually a good night's rest.

Family challenges

With some experience behind me, I felt that to have a settled and happy home was essential before beginning the work. It was clear that we were going to be exposed to a variety of pressures.

We had arrived in Soho too late to have the advantage of a choice of secondary schools for Jon. Our move into central London had meant leaving his beloved Colfe's School. The only option was a school in Paddington, where he was one of only six English speaking boys in a class of thirty-six. The Head teacher was a 'super head' in his day, but the school left a great deal to be desired. Its redeeming feature was an enthusiastic, smoking, sports master who ran football and cricket teams on Saturdays. As a keen goalie and wicket keeper, Jon got thoroughly involved, eventually playing for the West London Schools' team. There were anxieties too. Boys from another local school invaded the play area and bullied the first years into handing over money and pens. Jon was one of the victims, losing his fare home and school pens.

Back in Soho, we waited for his return. He should have been home by 5 pm. But where was he? The bus should have brought him to Oxford Street, from where he could safely walk down Regent Street and into Carnaby Street, where either Pam or I would meet him, and walk home together. There were also dangers closer to home.

The front door of our flats had no security and anyone could slip inside, come down the steps and do whatever they wanted in the dark recesses.

It was a public toilet and a convenient place for prostitutes to entertain their customers; bag-snatchers would slip in to sort out what they wanted from their booty, dumping the rest; and it was also a safe place for rough sleepers, both men and women, to rest, leaving their filthy blankets, rubbish and worse, behind them. All good reasons for seeing Jon safely indoors at the end of the school day.

On the night in question, Jon arrived home at 7.30 pm, having worked out the general direction, and walking the parts of the bus route he recognized. He still remembers arriving home on another evening, later than usual, and while making his way down the steps into the gloom of the basement being confronted by a bag-woman (a homeless woman who carries all her possessions in a shopping bag). She yelled at him out of the shadows. Terrified, he ran back out into the street, afraid to come home until he was sure the coast was clear.

Meanwhile, Lois faced challenges of her own. A pharmacy student at a college in Gray's Inn Road, she travelled by the underground each day. On one occasion, she, like other female passengers no doubt, was 'flashed' by one of the dubious characters who spent their day travelling the underground system—presumably a better option than sitting in cold, damp doorways above ground. Lois reacted calmly (she was her mother's daughter!) and responded with withering humour: 'What do you call that?' then walked on by! There were also regular taunts and 'offers' from drivers cruising Soho streets while she was heading home from Oxford Circus Station. Lois learned to stick to the main roads, dodging into Soho only at the last minute.

I was beginning to realise that, by responding to the call to serve in Soho, I was subjecting the whole family to experiences Pam and the children ought not to have had to endure.

I was beginning to realise that, by responding to the call to serve in Soho, I was subjecting the whole family to experiences Pam and the children ought not to have had to endure

Out of the blocks

The recent months had been challenging, but within days of moving into the Dwellings, the real issue confronted us. The principles that were to guide the project were agreed long ago, but practically, where were we to begin?

Clearly there were priorities: first, the need to discover what went on in the community through a twenty-four-hour period; and, second, the need to begin visiting our immediate neighbours in the Marshall Street Dwellings.

Discovering what was going on in the community was never going to be a theoretical exercise. It would mean observing the area at all times of day and night. There were well-known organizations based in the area, like Centrepoint, the homeless charity, and Soho's last surviving primary school in Great Windmill Street, plus a variety of other special interest groups.

In 1982, Soho wasn't yet the twenty-four-hour place it is today. I soon discovered that the area seemed to re-invent itself at regular intervals during that period. Prior to the IRA's bombing campaign in London (Soho experienced incidents of this) the horses of the Household Cavalry were exercised along Piccadilly, often entering Soho via Great Windmill Street. It was a lovely sound to wake up to on those mornings, usually about 5 am. The 'barrow boys' began laying out their stalls in Berwick Street around 6 am, six days a week. From 8 am, large numbers of people employed in the area began spilling out of the underground stations at Oxford Circus and Piccadilly Circus, carrying their morning fix of coffee. Around 8.30 am there were sounds of children being led through the streets, heading for the school in Great Windmill Street. By 10 am the entire area began to heave with shoppers and day trippers. At lunch time the many sandwich bars and the squares were crowded with workers enjoying a mid-day break. The evening brought another change, with theatre-goers and diners crowding in. Apparently, eleven million people a year came to enjoy the West End theatres, queueing to see such productions as *The Mousetrap* and *The Phantom of the Opera*, both of which enjoyed long runs.

Entertainment—Soho style

Soho had its own brand of entertainment: brash, aggressive, and often threatening. Sex shops, sex cinemas and clubs, strip and peep shows and brothels dominated the central area.

Paul Raymond's empire was involved in a variety of dubious ventures. Known as the 'King of Porn' his public face was displayed most clearly in the seedy 'Review Bar' in Walker's Court. Entrance was limited to members only, but hopefuls could join by paying at the door. Its membership was said to number 45,000! Small and artificially tanned, Raymond could sometimes be seen in Soho streets, surrounded by a group of broad-shouldered men, while moving from one of his establishments to another. He became extremely wealthy, largely from his dealing in West End property, magazine publishing, and the sex industry. Later, he became a recluse following the death of his daughter Debbie from an overdose of cocaine. Reportedly worth £650 million, he died in 2008, aged 82.

I realised something of the scale of the sex industry in the area one evening when a policeman confided that there were ninety-two brothels within a two-minute stroll of where we were standing in Brewer Street. Although covering an area of little more than one square mile, for two hundred years Soho had been at the heart of London's sex industry. In the year of our arrival the number of premises involved in the sex trade, in one form or another, had reached one hundred and eighty-five. Although, with tighter laws and the more recent 'gentrification' of the area, this had dropped to thirty ten years later, Soho remains the centre for London's sex industry and gay community. Perhaps it is ironically appropriate that it was in Soho in 1854 that Dr John Snow famously discovered cholera to be a water-borne disease when he traced a cholera outbreak to a local Soho pump that was fed by an underground stream contaminated by raw sewage!

Soho had its own brand of entertainment: brash, aggressive, and often threatening. Sex shops, sex cinemas and clubs, strip and peep shows and brothels dominated the central area

Throw into the mix the casinos, Ronnie Scott's jazz club, dodgy bookshops, international restaurants, peep shows, photo booths, bars and fifty pubs which attracted a certain clientele, and you have a glimpse of Soho's night life in the early 1980s. Most establishments were closing down by 3 am, but that was the cue for the Westminster night team to begin sweeping the streets, hosing down the pavements—urine and vomit were inevitably part of the scene—and emptying the large rubbish bins.

Much later, when the Soho church had literature to distribute to every letter-box, there was just one sensible opportunity, between 5.00 and 7.00 in the morning!

Getting started

Night after night I returned home wondering how those involved in Soho's night life could ever be reached with the gospel. This question would have to wait until an active church was in place. First, I must get to meet Soho's five thousand real residents.

Where to begin? We had nineteen neighbours on our doorstep!

I remember taking the first step up the stairway which would take me to the top floor, and flats 17, 18, 19, and 20 of City of Westminster Dwellings. It was 10 am on a Monday, hopefully the most convenient time to find our neighbours at home. I was armed with a ballpoint pen, a small, wire-bound notebook, a dozen copies of a card introducing us as a family and sharing why we had come to make our home in Soho. I also had a slim Gideons' New Testament.

Our first Soho home. We moved into no.4 in the basement of The City of Westminster Dwellings, a Victorian block of twenty flats

We brightened up the basement with flowers

Since I had promised to give ten years to preparing the ground for establishing an indigenous local church, my essential policy was to build long-term relationships, while using every opportunity to share the Christian message whenever it occurred.

I kept in mind that more than one hundred years had passed since there had been an evangelical church in Soho, so our neighbours would never have experienced a visit like the one they were about to receive that October morning. Before the First World War, the area was served by a variety of Anglican and free churches. The building of one of them, a Congregational church, still occupies a site on a corner of Carnaby Street. Now part of the rag trade, it once seated two thousand people, and ran a day school for the children of the area.

> More than one hundred years had passed since there had been an evangelical church in Soho

The Great War of 1914–18 was life-changing in every way. Not only were there nearly a million British fatalities, it also brought about significant social change at home. Returning soldiers expected an improvement in living conditions. Families tended to move out of the inner-city areas, seeking larger and better accommodation in the suburbs. A Baptist congregation enjoyed the facility of a building in Soho, but that too fell into disuse. Therefore, our work began without a building or home to call our own. There was no congregation awaiting us. There was nothing! It all began with this Monday morning's attempt to meet our neighbours....

It turned out to be a morning for learning some facts about Soho residential life. Every door had a spy-hole through which the tenant could check who was at their door. The general rule was, if you don't recognize the caller, pretend not to be at home, certainly don't open the door. It was also generally true that neighbours had almost nothing to do with each other. There was little evidence of neighbours visiting each other or meeting socially. 'Better to keep yourself to yourself' seemed to be the rule; it was probably safer that way. The average age of our neighbours was high. The majority of the twenty homes were occupied by a single person, mainly women. There were several couples, but only one family with children apart from our own.

My small notebook began to contain useful information. I devised a system of note-making which was to prove invaluable in the long-term. Whatever the response, or none, was noted for further reference. NI indicated 'not in'; INO indicated 'in but not opening'; FW indicated 'friendly welcome'; PBO indicated 'polite brush off'; BO indicated 'brush off'. Occasionally, I was pleased to note, CA, 'call again'.

I quickly became convinced that, although there were significant risks involved, it was best for me to visit alone. To have one unknown person on the doorstep was daunting enough, but two would have been just too much. The risks were real, a wide variety of people, men and women, lived in these past-their-sell-by-date flats. It was unusual to be invited in at the first visit—only John at number 6 was pleased to renew the contact begun some weeks earlier. It may not have been a very productive morning of 'cold' calling, but I was not discouraged. It was the long-term contact which really produced the relationships I was trying to build.

> It was the long-term contact which really produced the relationships I was trying to build

Being resident in the Dwellings meant that we had the luxury of being in close contact with our neighbours, and were likely to meet them on the public stairway most days. In some ways, this kind of contact was more natural and productive. Sooner or later help would be needed, and we were the people willing and probably able to help on the spot.

The pattern for the wider visiting was emerging. After the Dwellings, I was eager to begin visiting the three tower blocks in the area: Blake House, Kemp House and Ingestre Court. Always short of breath, it made sense to take the lift to the top floor and work my way down by the stairs. The tower blocks were built more recently than the Marshall Street Dwellings, probably in the 1960s. I soon discovered that every block had its own personality and clientele.

I began with Blake House, Dufours Place, the closest to Marshall Street. The 'Blake' refers to William Blake, the eighteenth-century poet, painter and visionary, who was born on the site. Arriving at the main door, I made another discovery: visitors off the street were not welcome! The outer doors were securely locked and could only be opened by the occupiers of the flats above. It was hopeless trying to persuade a resident to release the door to a complete stranger. Some years later, when our own home was secured in this way, we too were unwilling to expose our own home, or our neighbour's, to callers we did not know. However, I discovered that there was a limited time in the mornings when the system allowed the postman and others making deliveries to gain entry and I took the liberty of using it.

This could have resulted in a fiery reception by residents, but the Lord was preparing a warm welcome for me. Still very new to this work, I hadn't yet started from the top, so arrived on the first floor. I was immediately greeted by frantic cries. A door was open, an elderly and very fragile lady was calling for help. Her toilet was blocked, and she had continued to flush it in the hope that everything would disappear. It didn't—but threatened to overflow! No-one else was responding, so I stepped in to help. Jacket off and sleeves rolled up, my prodding efforts were rewarded with a whoosh—and a cry of relief from the lady. 'Would you like to wash your hands?' 'Yes please.' 'Would you like a cup of tea?' 'Yes please.' 'What's your name?' the lady asked as she poured the tea. Her question answered, she began to share her Jewish origins. She had been born to

Russian parents who came to Britain to escape persecution in the 1880s. Like thousands of others, they settled in the East End of London, living in utter poverty, but eventually prospering and progressing to a home in the West End. It was an encouraging start to Blake House. There were other Jews living there, and they got to hear of the Christian who was willing to get his hands down the loo!

Later, when the team was in place, we responded to calls to lend Jews a hand with the preparation of their homes for certain festivals. Memories flood back to a home where Andrew and I dismantled a large complicated chandelier, composed of many pieces of crystal. These had to be taken down individually, washed in soapy water, and rinsed in clean water before being dried and polished with a soft cloth. Thinking back, I'm not entirely sure that the sparkling pieces were hung in precisely the right place but no complaint was ever made.

This kind of activity was hardly church planting, but bridges were being built, giving access to homes and the people who lived there. Friendships were being made, and trust was being strengthened, so a clear Christian witness was being made. The alternative was to remain locked out in the street. If someone I had already visited crossed the road to avoid meeting me again in the street, I would reckon that I had failed miserably in handling the initial contact.

Door to door visiting was still the daily task; there was little else I could do. Wherever people lived or worked, attempts were made to forge a link with them.

Behind the front doors

Mr Lewis (an adopted anglicized name) wasn't pleased that I knocked on his door. An elderly Jew, he took objection to a Christian calling on him. His anger was so fierce that I could say nothing to assure him that I was not targeting him but visiting everyone. I apologized for disturbing him and moved on to the next home. This was certainly a VBO ('violent brush off') in my notebook!

Thankfully there were others who appreciated my visits, so Mr Lewis and I sometimes met in the lift or on the landing. There were no further outbursts, just hard looks and deep mumbling. Then, late one winter's evening, I was heading for home along Broadwick Street when I saw someone in the shadows, crouching down and clutching at his chest. It was Mr Lewis. Thankfully he was almost home, so it was not difficult to get him into the building, up the lift and indoors. It was a recurring problem apparently, and he had the medication in his bathroom cabinet. With Mr Lewis safely in his chair, it was brought and taken. Within a few minutes the pain had passed and he was comfortable again. I stayed long enough to make sure he was safe to leave, then promised to visit again in the morning.

I was back, promptly at 10 am. I tapped on the door, which opened almost immediately, and was invited in. Mr Lewis was appreciative of the help given the previous evening and we eventually got round to talking about the Jewish faith; I think it was he who raised the subject. At one point, he went to a cupboard, and came back with a beautifully tailored waistcoat. I saw it had been ripped all down the front, across the heart, yet the rip was neatly tailored! My host explained that the waistcoat was worn to the synagogue on the Day of Atonement and signified the wearer's heart sorrow for sin. The Bible reference came to mind: 'Rend your heart and not your garments. Return to the LORD your God, for he is gracious and compassionate. Slow to anger and abounding in love' (Joel 2:13). Sadly, this was beyond my Jewish friend's understanding as he was steeped in the tradition of his religion, but a bridge had been built between us. Hopefully we could meet another day and continue the discussion.

Our next-door neighbour was one of the biggest men I had ever met. He was not fat or overweight, he was just BIG. I have since heard about 'Irish Giantism' and I suspect Patrick was an example of it. He had to duck his head and turn sideways to get through a normal door. He had been moved in next to us when the previous occupant, a lady, was thought to be in need of care. She was easy to live with, although she was always hanging around the front door in the hope of catching one of us as we left the home. We also knew she was listening when we used the telephone, which was situated just inside our front door. She began coming to our morning service, accompanied by her black and white cat who listened respectfully. Eventually she was moved on to somewhere more suitable.

Within a few days Patrick arrived, with the help of the social services team. Having a home help, who wasn't actually very helpful, Patrick didn't need to go out; everything was brought to him. I had a feeling the home help would rather do the shopping than spend time with Patrick. The home was in a shocking state. One Saturday night, having nothing to drink, Patrick made the effort to climb the stairs and was gone for several hours. Returning the worse for wear, he fell down the steps and lay at the bottom bleeding. It didn't look too serious so we got him inside, cleaned him up and put him to bed.

Checking on him the next morning, Patrick was hung over but none the worse for his adventure the previous evening. It seemed to me that not only was the home neglected but that he too was in a shocking state. I promised to call every Wednesday morning and shave him. If he had a mind to do it, he could stand at the sink and wash himself, but it would be unwise for him to risk handling a razor!

The door was never locked, so I could check him at any time. On the morning of the first shave I arrived and was pleased to find him sober and awake. I did notice that the rug in front of his chair was squelching with ... yes, it was urine! The shaving went well, given the circumstances, but I needed to improve on the plastic Bic razor. The arrangement continued on a weekly basis. Sometimes Patrick was awake and ready for action, while on other days he was in bed, fast asleep, wrapped in an alcoholic haze.

Ben was another of our basement neighbours, an elderly, dignified West Indian, partially paralysed down one side. Ben had a routine. On certain mornings, he climbed the steps with great difficulty and made his way along Marshall and Broadwick Streets, heading for the market. There he bought off-cuts of meat that were probably not normally for sale in the window. We suspected that Ben was well known to the butcher, and that he was either given, or bought these scraps for almost nothing. At home, they were put into a black metal pot and boiled on the gas stove. Ben rarely asked for anything, except for a couple of tea bags to drop into a tall, filthy, metal jug where many old bags were collecting in the bottom. It was then topped up with boiling water.

There was another need, which we took upon ourselves to resolve. Ben's toilet was in the passage, not inside his front door, like the rest. Ben made no effort to keep the area even reasonably clean and the stench was sufficient to have the residents on the floors above complaining during our first summer. It was true they didn't have to live with it, but they did have to come down to ground level when leaving or entering the building. Pam and I felt we should do what we could. We invested in a broom with tough bristles, a bucket and a large bottle of disinfectant. The problem didn't just lie within the toilet bowl, but up the walls and on the floor. Having begun within the toilet, it was necessary to clean throughout the passage, sweeping the filthy water out of the back door.

During one Saturday morning clean-up, I slipped indoors to get my camera. The shot I took of the offending toilet, before and after our efforts, and another of Pam, in silhouette, sweeping filthy water out of the building, became a popular slide when used in deputation meetings. Today it might have gone viral.

We reaped a harvest of appreciation from our fellow residents. Suspicion was dispersed, just like the offensive stench when confronted by the

Pam's regular task to scrub and disinfect around our front door, frequently used as a public toilet by rough sleepers, drunks and prostitutes, otherwise neighbours complained about its stench

cleansing bleach earlier in the morning. We owed so much to that broom, bucket and big bottle of bleach. It opened doors, mouths, and even hearts. Candidates for the ministry aren't taught this in college.

We owed so much to that broom, bucket and big bottle of bleach. It opened doors, mouths, and even hearts. Candidates for the ministry aren't taught this in college

Ben's life ended sadly. A smart young woman used to visit him on Friday evenings. One evening, receiving no reply, she knocked on our door. I checked the rear window. Ben was lying across the gas fire in the dark room. Rookie PC Scott, arrived, and said he ought to go in alone as there might have been foul play. There was a full investigation, concluding that Ben had died of natural causes.

Not all my contacts were elderly, frail or Jewish. When visiting one of the more modern blocks of flats one Wednesday morning, the door was opened by a pleasant, fair haired woman. She smiled, and said she recognized me from the photograph in the Soho Society's *Clarion* magazine. Once inside the home, I was offered a comfortable chair and a cup of coffee. In fact, cups of coffee kept on being served during the next two and a half hours! Sadie was Polish, and obviously lacked someone, anyone, to talk to. Several times I said I should really be going, and even stood up to leave more than once, only to find Sadie had something else she really needed to share. Eventually, I made it to the door and out onto the landing. Sadie was still talking as I headed for the stairwell, head buzzing with an overload of information.

During lunch there was a telephone call from a contact I had got to know well in the same block. 'I'm just phoning to warn you, Michael, that the police have been called by Sadie. Her gold Cartier watch has gone missing. I'll keep you up to date with any developments.' My heart sank. I felt it best to give the whole thing over to the Lord and stay at home in case the police wanted to check me out. I hadn't too long to wait. Another call from the first caller explained that only two people had been to the home that morning: me, and Sadie's brother. Fortunately, the brother admitted his offense. He was an alcoholic, and while Sadie was making him a sandwich he had rifled through a drawer and pocketed the watch.

I was in the clear. I realised that visiting was a risky business, and that it would take just one false step to wreck both one's reputation and the entire project.

Holidays?

As the first summer arrived, we struggled with the question of if and when it would be appropriate to take a holiday away from Soho? Part of the commitment to our work was to live with and live like the people we were attempting to reach with the gospel. Since we were living among some of the poorest people in the community, the answer to the holiday question seemed to be: never. However, we were living on the job, and therefore at everyone's beck-and-call, at any time of the day and night. The need was also developing to travel on deputation work, to encourage churches all over the country to pray for us and support us financially if possible. Then there was also the pressure of limited space and facilities in our home. Was it so unreasonable to seek a week or two each year to enjoy somewhere where there was hot water on tap, a bath or shower available at any time? Besides, we had committed ourselves to work for ten years, so wasn't it important to remain strong to complete this undertaking?

Weighing these issues, and thinking of the wider local population, we noticed that many of our Italian, Spanish, Portuguese, Irish and other neighbours regularly returned to their native country in August. Some of the shops were closed for this period in the 1980s.

We eventually accepted that a two-week summer holiday was justified. Thankfully, we were never short of kind offers of accommodation in various parts of the country, while homeowners were away themselves or had space to spare. Once Lois and Jon became independent of us, Pam and I travelled abroad each summer, hoping for peace, quiet, and sunshine!

Returning from two lovely weeks in Malta we found Wally sitting on our steps. He had discovered when we would be home. Wally and his wife, Eileen, were living in the Dwellings when I first began to visit. They didn't give me the time of day, a complete BO. It wasn't a happy home.

Eileen regularly left the flats to go shopping, with a scarf covering half of her face and the black eye she had received during one of Wally's drunken outbursts. Sometime earlier, the couple had been offered a new home, a flat overlooking Charing Cross Road. We had met up again when I came across them while visiting the new development.

Wally stood up to greet us, smiling. 'I need your help', he started. Pam sensed this could be a long job and suggested that we got the luggage down into the flat first. I re-joined Wally in the street. He had responded to an advertisement which offered an exchange: a rented, three-bedroomed house near Windsor, for a one-bedroomed flat in Central London. Everyone had agreed to the swap, a date had been fixed, and today was the day for Wally to move out, and to move into the new home. Where did I fit in I wondered? Wally had sorted his furniture, hired a van but had no money to pay for it. He was also banned from driving for drink-driving. Would I step up to the plate for both these, and lend a hand with the lifting and carrying at both ends? Given the circumstances, what could I do? The woman intending to swap with Wally and Eileen was waiting to move in as we spoke.

With the cash paid, the van hired and loaded, we travelled to Windsor. The van was unloaded, driven back to London and returned to the hire company. I arrived home at 11.30pm. All was quiet as I undressed, and clambered to the other side of a sleeping Pam. Thinking back to our home-coming earlier in the day, the incident involving Wally and Eileen confirmed that we should certainly take a break for two weeks every summer if we were going to see the ten years through.

Life below ground

Not only were we beginning to feel more at home in our basement flat but also beginning to see why the Lord had provided this home for us. Wasn't he Lord and God of all? It would have been a small thing for him to provide a home for us in one of the smartest tower blocks, or even a pent house by the Ritz, overlooking Green Park, but we were offered the keys to 4 City of Westminster Dwellings.

The quality of life was improving. Attempts had been made to create a shower in the toilet area. It worked by fitting a plastic folding door where the original door had been. Slide open the door, and there were two steps up, making it possible to walk across the lid that covered the shower tray when not in use. Then, two steps down to floor level. Using the toilet required turning round with care. To exit, simply reverse the procedure, passing the minute wall mounted basin, just deep enough to rinse your fingers. Eventually, the shower had to be abandoned for washing in the kitchen sink because the waste water of the entire block flowed down to the basement, some of it flooding back into our shower tray.

On balance we felt it was more important to sit comfortably in flat-pack chairs bought from John Lewis, rather than sitting at a small dining table on upright chairs. It meant eating our meals off our laps but it solved the problem of where to seat family and visitors to the home. We invested in four folding chairs, which would also accommodate those attending a home group. They could easily be stacked under a bed when not in use.

These improvements must have been effective, because when a senior colleague's wife came to visit from the suburbs she pronounced the flat to be: 'Sweet. Just like living in a caravan.'

Only rarely were there tensions over our living conditions, but the strain showed itself unexpectedly one evening. We were invited for a meal with colleagues recently arrived in London. They lived in the manse in one of the most expensive areas of London. There was much to impress. Lovely street, quality house, and all the space a family of four would ever need. We felt like the poor relations. We were made welcome and were served a first-class meal. Later we began to compare notes on our respective moves into the city. Suddenly our host's two teenage children burst into the room, arguing furiously over who was going to have which room for their bedroom, although there were rooms to spare. Pam burst into tears. It all seemed so petty compared with our life at home, with nineteen-year-old Lois, and twelve-year-old Jon sharing a basement box room. But it was all over in a moment and was never mentioned again.

Visitors to the basement

As the months passed, a variety of people began to visit us at home. Some from other churches came to look at where we were living, and how we were approaching the work. As Christians, most were relaxed and their visit encouraged us. Occasionally, local people called to share confidential things, which meant the rest of the family either retreating to a bedroom, standing up in the kitchen, or going window shopping in Regent Street until the interview was over.

Occasionally, lovely things happened. Like the evening when two young men arrived unannounced. They had heard that Christians had come to live in Soho and were attempting to establish a new church, so they came to say, 'Hello.' They lived in Brighton and travelled to London each evening because they were part of the cast of 'Evita' which was playing at one of the West End theatres. Madonna was the lead singer! They were Christians, and wanted to identify with what we were doing. They produced a tin containing a beautiful Dundee cake, which we shared before they had to rush off to 'make up' for the evening performance! We never met them again.

Another unexpected visitor arrived one Sunday morning. Sitting together in the living room we heard the clanging of a metal chain against the railings outside and looking up we saw a cyclist, totally wrapped up against the cold. Two minutes later there was a knock at the door. The cyclist, still wrapped up, said nothing but thrust a package into my hands.

Then he was gone. Was it safe to open the package? We did. It contained nothing more dangerous than £500 in £20 notes. There was no letter, and no name—no-one to thank but the Lord!

Not all our visitors were such a blessing! A young man turned up unannounced one Thursday morning. I had received some disturbing information about him since leaving Thamesmead. For some years he had been the Treasurer of the Area 3 Residents Association. He seemed to have a working knowledge of accounting, but I had heard that when it came to auditing the books they didn't balance, and several thousand pounds were missing. I kept what I knew to myself and let my visitor talk on. He claimed to be an accountant for a major airline, and that he was in town for an important meeting. I felt it was time to interrupt him and share what I knew about the situation: he was no longer able to remain in Thamesmead, his wife had ejected him from the home and he had nowhere to go. Rather than come clean and ask for help, he couldn't wait to get outside and away towards Carnaby Street. We never saw him again either.

In some ways, the most challenging, yet rewarding, visit involved Margaret, from the top floor of the Dwellings. Andrew and I used to meet with several other evangelical Christians at St Dunstan's Church, Fleet Street, to pray before the working week began. We were a mixed group, including an industrialist, a lawyer and others involved in different areas of Christian ministry. Arriving home around 9.30 am, I looked down into our flat through railings. In a chair by the window sat Margaret from number 19, wrapped in a candlewick bedspread. I had met her on the first morning when visiting the Dwellings and had been given a 'PBO'. She was polite enough but had still given me a brush off. This could be interesting.

Pam opened the front door and whispered that there had been trouble. There was no brush off this time; Margaret was eager to share her experience. She had been widowed some years before and had met partner Len while dancing at the Hammersmith Palais. He wasn't in the first flush of youth and had a lifestyle which didn't help his moves on the dance floor, but his greying hair was sleek, and his moustache neatly trimmed. He danced well. Margaret eventually gave up her home and moved in with Len. She carried on with her job with London Transport, earning the income which kept the rent paid and Len in drink. Eight years on they were still together, but it was about to end.

Margaret had come home on the previous Friday evening to find Len the worse for drink. Resenting that she had been away from the home for so long, he locked the door and told her she would be staying indoors for the weekend. They got through Saturday and Sunday, but by Monday morning there was nothing to smoke or drink. The newsagent, a few yards down Marshall Street, would be open at 8 am, so Margaret was sent out to get supplies, in her night-wear, and with a candlewick bedspread wrapped around her to prevent her escaping. Feeling it was time to get out of this relationship and an opportunity to escape the home, she knocked on our door. She needed help to get away.

Margaret repeated the story she had already shared with Pam. She had some good friends who would take her in, but all her clothes and other belongings were upstairs! What was to be done? Prayer was the priority, then practical help. I offered to accompany Margaret to the flat. While I engaged with Len, she would dress, pack, and we would leave together. We were climbing the stairs when Margaret said, 'Watch out for the knives.' Knives! What knives? When Margaret arrived home on Friday Len had put a coffee table in front of his chair and placed three knives on it, within easy reach. The front door was ajar. We walked down the hall, Margaret was behind me. I pushed open the living room door.

Len looked up, surprised, and struggled to his feet. We stood looking each other in the eye. Neither of us spoke. The knives—Crocodile Dundee style—were on the table between us. It was Len who blinked first, crumpling back into the chair, sobbing. By this time Margaret was dressed, and with bags roughly packed she was standing outside on the landing. I struck a deal with Len before leaving: let Margaret go, don't try to trace her, and I would visit him every day, and support him through this bout of drinking. Agreed? Agreed!

I visited the home every day for three months, stripping a drenched bed, washing up the pile of crockery in the sink, making sure Len had food and tea—but no alcohol. I also undertook to persuade our local GP to visit to give him a health-check. Each visit ended with an attempt to share relevant Bible promises and prayer. Len gradually recovered to the point of managing the home himself, and even beginning to make short excursions outside. I still remember my final visit. Len said he thought he had done so well in getting back to normal life once again. He made it clear he didn't need my help, my Bible or my prayers now, and wouldn't be expecting me to call again. He escorted me to the door, locking it behind me, making the point. Over the next few months there were telephone calls from the hospital and the police station. Would I go and see, or collect, him? Eventually, Len died, still drinking, and still living at the expense of another woman.

On that Monday morning, I found Margaret downstairs waiting to speak to me. She asked, 'Michael, is it right that you invite people to your home and teach them the Bible?' I told her that several of us met on Tuesday evenings at 7.30 pm. We were learning about the Sermon on the Mount. 'Could I come?' she requested. I assured her she would be very welcome, and that I would make sure she got into the building safely, and out again at the end of the evening.

It was six weeks later when Margaret shared that she had put her faith in Jesus as her Saviour and Lord, and could she be baptized? She spoke of the difference having faith in Jesus had made to her: he had forgiven her past, given her a new beginning, and now, she was able to look at herself in the mirror, a new woman in Christ and no longer ashamed!

There were few incidents that were threatening, but Pam did have an unpleasant experience when opening the front door one Saturday afternoon, planning to go shopping. Four young men were standing on the basement steps, inside the front door—urinating through the railings around our front door. She calmly reminded them that people lived here, it was their home, and that there was a public toilet in nearby Broadwick Street. For some reason, this was a red rag to the boys who shouted filthy abuse, and charged down the steps towards her. Whatever the short-comings of the Dwellings, they each possessed a strong front door. Pam was quick enough to step back inside and slam the door before the mob arrived. After some kicking and hammering on the door they left.

Later, one of Pam's most important jobs was to hang around the telephone, outside the study door, when threatening visitors came into the home. This was just in case police support was needed. From 1989 when she was Minister for the Department of Health, Virginia Bottomley closed the ring of large Victorian mental institutions around London in preference for care for the mentally ill in the community. Several of these were resettled in Soho; they were all young. I got to know a young schizophrenic who came to our home occasionally. Drug dealers soon took advantage of him and used his flat as a base. One afternoon he called for no obvious reason. At first we chatted calmly about issues in general, but then he began to tense up, clenching his fists and pace around the room. Suddenly he blurted out, 'Michael, I don't know whether to admire you, or kill you.' He looked at me for a moment then rushed out of the flat, crashing the doors shut as he went. I once received an envelope through the post. It contained printed material advertising the most degrading pornography. It ended with a handwritten warning: 'Do not pass this on to the Police.' I did.

To complete the story of the occupants of the four basement flats. At Number 1 lived two Irishmen. For most of their working lives they had worked as 'navvies'. They were now retired, quiet, polite, very fond of Guinness, and so broadly Irish that we could scarcely understand a word they said.

49 Moving forward

The work in Soho was slow. Those who enjoy a rich church life, with its teaching and fellowship, have entered into the faithfulness and hard work of earlier generations. Starting from nothing is like getting your 'dead' car to move. All the effort goes into getting the wheels to turn, just a little. Once the car is moving, it is comparatively easy to push it forward. It was said of the mighty but flawed Samson: 'He will begin the deliverance of Israel from the hands of the Philistines' (Judges 13:5). All credit to Samson because that was the tough part. It left an easier task for others to achieve the complete liberty of God's chosen people. The initial work in Soho was always going to involve reaching out before we could hope to draw in those who showed an interest in discovering more of the good news.

By early 1983 I knew that it wasn't enough to say to those I met on the doorstep that we planned to hold a Sunday morning service sometime in the future, we now had to organize it, and get on with it. But where could we find a meeting space? Our living room would only seat 6, if no-one moved. The Charles Norton Centre in Broadwick Street was run by Age Concern. It may have resembled a dated care home in terms of the carpet and furniture, but it could be free for us to use on Sunday mornings for £10 a week. It was also in just the right place, at the base of Blake House.

So, four months after arriving in the area, we began to meet for an hour, with coffee afterwards. The group was small: us, a family of four; Chris, the daughter of the family who lived next door to us in Thamesmead, now living in London, and several individuals and a couple, who were members of churches supporting the project. Two of them were pianists, which contributed a great deal to the services in the early days.

We invested in *New International Version* Bibles and *Grace* hymn books. Both these were ground-breaking at the time. In parallel with the policy of living with the people and living like the people, we needed to shape the worship and teaching to the needs and understanding of those who came to join us. Eventually, I sensed tension among the Christians who came to us from other churches; they reasonably expected us to develop the service along traditional lines and not according to the simple needs of the newcomers. Over a five-year period, with the helpfulness of growing numbers and the arrival of several Christian students who looked on us as their spiritual home while in London, we became a more local congregation.

> In parallel with the policy of living with the people and living like the people, we needed to shape the worship and teaching to the needs and understanding of those who came to join us

Our congregation

We had the use of the Norton Centre for about ten years, time enough for an extraordinary number of characters to join us—or pass through.

Mr Peacock lived in Blake House, just above our meeting place. He offered a 'COI' ('come on in') welcome when I visited. He was elderly and had teeth which had a life of their own! The home was a replica of the tenant himself, eccentric, eclectic and entertaining. Mr Peacock claimed to be a 'spiritual healer'—extending his gnarled hands for his visitor to admire. I didn't press him to say whether he was a Christian with a gift of healing, or one of the 'spiritualist' sort. Apparently, it wasn't only humans he healed, but animals too. I never did get the opportunity to question the horse which had benefited from Mr Peacock's healing touch, but Mr P began coming to the service regularly, entertaining us at coffee time with his 'honky-tonk' style of piano playing.

Laura also was a resident in the flats above the Norton Centre. There was no welcome into the home at first, but she was happy to talk on the doorstep. Laura was Italian by birth, a devout Roman Catholic, and a member of the historic Warwick Street Church, Our Lady of the Assumption & St Gregory. Physically fragile, she regularly attended the

Chapter 5

daily Mass, making her way to the church through the tourist areas without fail. Later I found her story moving when she shared it while drinking tea in her home one afternoon. She was a teenager during Italy's troubled years. Her parents were casualties of the fighting, and as a teenager she was shipped out to Nazi Germany and trained as a nurse. She spoke of the day when, with all members of the staff, she was instructed to change her uniform, do her hair, and report in the entrance hall of the hotel which served as a make-shift hospital. A large black Mercedes-Benz car drew up outside the main door, and the Führer himself strode into the building. He made his way down the line, from the senior staff to the ward nurses, congratulating them on their service. Laura said Hitler eventually arrived in front of her, put his hand on her shoulder and said, 'Laura, thank you, and well done.'

I'm still amazed at her story, and how a lone Italian woman could survive the war, escape the chaos of cities reduced to rubble, find her way through Europe to England into this small, central London community, and still be here many years later—and in our congregation.

Jonathan arrived one Sunday morning. The service was well under way when he pushed his way through the door and sat quietly, listening. When approached immediately after the closing prayer, two things were clear: he was South African, and he was hung-over. He admitted having had a drink, but said he needed it. His girlfriend, who lived with him in a flat above, had died of a severe asthma attack the previous evening. An ambulance had been called but she couldn't be revived. He drank some coffee, then left for home. I promised to call on him the following morning.

When I arrived at Number 2 the door was open, swinging in the breeze. The lock was broken. No-one responded to my call, so I went in. It was a bed-sit and Jonathan was deeply asleep. The smell of alcohol was everywhere. By the side of the bed, a glass-topped table lay smashed on the floor, no doubt the result of Jonathan falling on it. Shattered glass and blood were everywhere. Clearly Jonathan was in no shape to have that talk I promised him. Should I leave him and come back later in the day? No, there was stuff to do. I cleared the crushed table and glass, washed the floor of its blood and the vomit I hadn't seen at first. Thankfully the flat was well off for disinfectant, cloths, and mops. These were the only sign that a woman had lived there. In the bathroom there was a pile of quality shirts, the kind bought in Jermyn Street. These had been soiled, a side-line of drinking to excess. I ran hot water into the bath, squeezed in anything which would disinfect and clean, then added the shirts. I checked Jonathan. He was still asleep. Thinking the shirts had had time to soak, I pummelled them, rinsed them in clean water, then hung them on the balcony to dry.

When I came back into the room, Jonathan was awake, leaning on one elbow, blinking in the sunlight. 'Who are you?' he asked. I explained that we had met downstairs in the service the previous morning, and that I had promised to come and talk with him today. Jonathan looked around and expressed surprise that the mess had been cleaned up and that his filthy shirts were hanging, drying in the sun. I told him this is what Christians do for those who need help. It was nothing out of the ordinary. He said, that in South Africa, daily services in the chapel were all part of public school life, but the ministers never did things like this.

Gradually his story emerged. His father was a millionaire industrialist, and Jonathan had been educated at a good public school before enrolling at a military training college. As a professional soldier he had reached the rank of captain and served his time. Already drinking heavily, a gap had opened up between himself and his family, and he had drifted to England and London. There was no mention of the woman who was supposed to have died in the flat over the weekend. I suspected she may have existed only in an alcoholic dream.

Jonathan was a reader. I began to feed him with Christian books which I hoped would lay the foundation for believing in Christ. For several weeks he was 'dry' but was more inclined to call at our home than join us regularly on Sunday or mid-week. When he first began to call, I made it a rule that he would not be invited in if he arrived worse for drink. I felt that this was fair to us as a family, and also good for our neighbours. Late one night, Jonathan arrived obviously drunk, and made a scene outside our home when I reminded him of the agreement. To keep a measure of control, I let him in. Under his arm he carried several of the books I had lent him. He threw them down on the floor and angrily announced that he wouldn't be reading them again. What was the problem? Apparently, it was Luke 9:23 that caused the trouble. Jesus demanded just too much of those who would follow him: 'If anyone would come after me, he must deny himself and take up his cross daily and follow me.' Jonathan may well have read these words through an alcoholic haze, and found them more easy to reject than the call of the bottle. Before leaving noisily, Jonathan made it clear that it wasn't only the books he was casting off, but we Christians who were trying to encourage him. I thought it best to let time pass before visiting him at home. When I did call, the door was still without a lock of any kind, and the flat was empty. Unknown to me, the rent hadn't been paid and the bailiffs had eventually ejected him from the home. I never heard anything of Jonathan again. Disappointments in church planting are usually deeper than in an established church.

> Disappointments in church planting are usually deeper than in an established church

Our neighbours

The last three years in our Marshall Street flat were seriously challenging. Immediately above us lived a really pleasant, middle-aged widow. Always beautifully dressed, her white hair (with its hint of blue) always in place, she actually enhanced the building. If only the rest of us were as impressive. One morning she knocked on the door to say she had been offered a flat in a smart tower block overlooking Lord's Cricket Ground in St John's Wood. We said we would miss her but hoped she would be very happy in her new home. We wondered who would be filling the new vacancy upstairs. We weren't left to wonder too long!

Mal McGirr, our housing manager, never admitted to being a man of God but, whether he was aware of it or not, he was certainly used by God. Not only did he allocate housing for us as a family, but Andrew Murray was also accommodated in 1986 when joining the team. Later, when a young member needed accommodation, her marriage having broken down, Mr McGirr responded positively to Pam's pleading on her behalf and provided a secure home for her in Westminster.

Within days of losing our upstairs neighbour, Mr McGirr called to share the news that a couple of new residents were going to be re-housed in the vacant flat. They had been living in a block just north of Oxford Street, but there had been a fire and they needed emergency accommodation. Professional etiquette prevented him from sharing the whole situation, but he cleverly said enough to enable us to read between the lines—brace yourselves!

There was a fair amount of banging and scraping as our new neighbours settled in, with help, during the first day, but this didn't remotely prepare us for what was to happen later that night. It was well after the pub's closing time when we woke with a start. The sound of singing in the street—or was it howling, or scolding? Whatever the sound, it increased horribly as the couple arrived outside our bedroom window. There was a fumbling with keys at the front door, arguments as they climbed the steps to their flat, and a great deal of stomping from one room to another as they tried to sort out who was going to sleep where. There was a thud as a heavy shoe was hurled across the room. We waited for the other to follow, but it didn't. This was a gentle introduction to life with our new neighbours for the next three years. Charlie and Florrie had arrived.

Florrie, the wife of Charlie, was expert at tagging a tourist for a contribution to her whisky addiction

Chapter 5

Picture Florrie, posing outside the Dwellings. She was in her 70s, draped in a dress down to her ankles, with a shawl around her shoulders. Her most striking feature was her long greying, matted hair, piled high on the top of her head. Charlie was of similar age, a 'will-o-the-wisp' in build, usually seen out and about in his singlet. Their relationship was brittle. At home, it took little to send them into total rage and conflict, day or night. No doubt, drink lay behind a great deal of the trouble. In Soho, Florrie was now in her element. With tourists packing the streets she used her skills, fine-tuned over many years, to fleece them of their money. She wasn't beyond using her appearance, apparent poverty, or foul-mouthed threats, to get the money for the next miniature bottle of whisky. The reaction of local shopkeepers was interesting. They didn't want her in their shop at any cost, even preferring to part with a bottle at a loss, just to get her to move on.

Charlie was his own character. Most weeks we had some entertainment at his expense. Our rubbish bins were emptied at 2 am on Wednesdays, a noisy business at the best of times. But the sound of bins being collected, mechanically wound up and emptied into the van, plus the sound of the good-natured banter of the bin-men was enough to light Charlie's fuse. If he was capable of stumbling out into the road after the night's drinking, he would appear in his underwear and singlet, complete with his boxing gloves on a string around his neck. I couldn't be bothered to get out of bed to watch, but Pam did, and was rewarded with a scene she remembered, and laughed about, for many years. Gloves on, Charlie was challenging the bin-men to a fight. They laughed and told him to go back to bed. When he didn't respond, one of the men squared up to him in mock challenge. Charlie quickly removed his gloves, throwing them around his neck on the string, staggering backwards from the weight of them and only just avoiding falling flat on his back. The men laughed and moved on down the street.

There were few nights in the next three years when we weren't disturbed by drunken brawling. Very soon, a walking stick became a necessity: we would whack the ceiling and shout, 'Charlie, get to sleep!'

It was inevitable that other tenants were also enraged by the nightly disturbances. We were advised by the Housing Department to keep a record of events over the next three months, a common delaying tactic. The record was soon full to overflowing but nothing was done. The City of Westminster Dwellings in Marshall Street were the end of the line; there was nowhere else for folk like Charlie and Florrie to go. I tried to help by visiting the home, taking care to refuse offers of a cup of tea. Charlie had been decorating the living room with the full colour pages of a pornographic magazine. We often drank tea at 2 am because we couldn't sleep. One evening I could be seen walking home with Florrie on my arm! She had been loitering in a shocking state. When I came indoors my family kept me at arm's length until I had washed and changed my clothes.

Life in the Dwellings was eventful, and it was a great place for discovering the realities of urban church planting. The Thamesmead experience had been a helpful prelude, but I quickly discovered it was unwise to move from one project to another and expect to transfer methods of working automatically. Those three months spent standing in doorways and walking the streets at all times of the day and night, were foundational to understanding how best to work.

> I quickly discovered it was unwise to move from one project to another and expect to transfer methods of working automatically

Friends in a 'cleaner' world

An increasing number of contacts in the wider community were made and developed. Among the first were the police officers based at West End Central, Savile Row, who pounded the Soho beat. During the three and a half years we spent in the Dwellings, we built good relationships with three men in particular. One, a sergeant, organized transport and helped with the lifting and carrying when we eventually moved into the Brewer Street accommodation. It was good to know they were around. For their part they were pleased to call in to check how we were and, of course, a cup of tea was always welcome.

There were occasions when neighbours in conflict needed the intervention of an authority figure. One neighbour, with a serious gambling habit, was illegally sub-letting a room in his flat. A furious row developed when the lodger was accused of falling behind in his agreed rent. He had a sheet of paper on which his payments were listed, apparently acknowledged with a signature. But was it forged? I wasn't able to resolve the issue, but I knew a man who could. The sergeant willingly sat in on a meeting with the tenant and lodger, and having checked specimens of handwriting, judged the signatures to be genuine. The situation became complicated by the discovery that the lodger was an illegal immigrant. Granted bail, he disappeared into the vast crowds of the West End. One interesting outcome of the contact with these beat officers was an invitation to tour the police station. An Inspector showed me round, introducing me to other policemen and women who had an input into the security of the West End.

Another relationship gave me particular encouragement. In nearby Poland Street, contact was made with an amazing group of Christian men and women—photographers, graphic designers, and copywriters—who were largely responsible for producing the impressive Tear Fund magazine. They were all members of various London churches. They invited me to join them each Wednesday for lunch, followed by a Bible study, all within an hour. We worked our way through the story of Samson, followed by a lively discussion and a question and answer session. I remember one bright, young Christian sharing how he resented his flat mates helping themselves to his sugar, and never replacing what they had used. Having prayed about it, he concluded a Christian should re-fill the bowl without complaint and make it available for all to use. Eventually, massive rising rental costs led to the team having to vacate the premises and find accommodation elsewhere.

Another valued opportunity opened up at the Sun-Life Insurance Company in Shaftesbury Avenue. Such opportunities came either through the project being mentioned in the Christian press, a deputation visit to a church, or because of our *inContact* circular being put through the office letter-box. A group of nine or ten Christians met each Thursday at lunch-time to share a Bible study with the group leader or an invited speaker. Being local, I was a regular guest. This contact eventually led to the Directors asking if I would investigate all the charities working in Soho, discovering their policies, the nature of their work, and their financial needs. Armed with this information, the Directors then allocated money for those I recommended being worthy of support. I was amazed at how much money was raised by these charities— and the size of the staff salaries paid!

Another regular engagement was with the Christian group which met at the Department of the Environment in Victoria. I was invited to update the group on the Soho project once or twice a year over the first ten years. The group was chaired by the civil servant who represented the British Government at any EU policy-debates on water. More challenging than these meetings were the three occasions when I was invited to be the speaker at the Department's Annual Carol Service. This was held in one of the church buildings in the area, and always attracted a large congregation, including the Government minister at the time, John Selwyn Gummer, and his fur-clad wife. On another of these occasions, I was shown into the vestry, where the resident clergyman prayed before we joined the congregation. He was Richard Chartres, who later became the Bishop of London. The guidance given to the speaker on these occasions was straightforward: don't exceed your allotted time of twenty minutes, and preach the gospel. I happily agreed to both.

6.9 Life above ground

Our time as tenants 'below ground' of City of Westminster Dwellings was coming to an end. It had been an eventful and valuable three and a half years. Apparently, our work in the area had been both noticed and appreciated, as had the fact that Jon and Lois had been sharing a single room. The Soho Housing Association was formed in 1977, to provide for the accommodation needs of local people particularly. We were offered a three-bedroomed flat in St James' Residences, Brewer Street, with central heating, hot water and a fully functioning bathroom! Previously known as 'Rogues Court', it was situated opposite 'Girls, Girls, Girls!', so once again we found ourselves in appropriate company for our work.

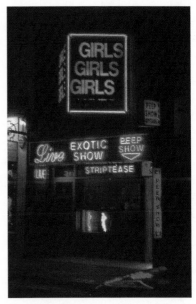

'St James' Residences' had undergone a radical renovation several years before, updating the flats for 1980s living. Previously, shared bathrooms were situated in the basement. I soon got to hear about some of the things that went on down there in those days. The individual toilets were originally situated outside each flat, in a cupboard-like space, on an attractive cast iron balcony. The balconies remained, but the toilets were now part of the

Our home in St James' Residences in Brewer Street was immediately opposite GIRLS GIRLS GIRLS

bathroom, inside each flat. The Residences were basically two elongated brick-built blocks arranged around a courtyard. Five stairways led to five levels of flats, with twenty flats on each floor, totalling sixty homes of various size.

Access to the Residences was through an arch fronting Brewer Street and protected by an electronically secured, large metal gate. A service room housed two tall bins where domestic waste was sorted and deposited, to be collected in the early hours of each Tuesday morning. Next door was a small laundry room with a washing machine and a spin dryer. A Family Centre for pre-school children occupied the basement, where the baths had been previously.

Flat 26 was on the first floor. The main bedroom and study overlooked the Soho Parish school playground, and eye-balled the windows of private flats situated in Great Windmill Street a few yards away. The remaining bedroom overlooked the courtyard. The living room had a single window

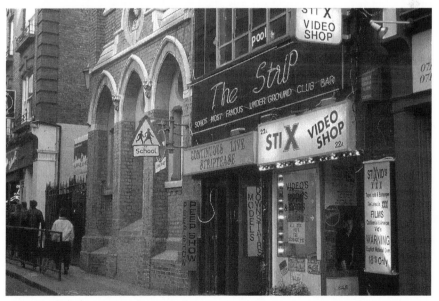

Our bedroom in St James' Residences overlooked Soho Parish School in Great Windmill Street. This became our new base for Sunday worship in 1993. Brothels were situated either side of the school gate

which looked out over the back of the flats and the small garden. There had of course been previous occupiers of the flat. Its condition was tired and in need of complete redecoration. The bathroom had no natural ventilation so an extractor fan was installed. This used air was expelled through a boxed pipe which ran through the living room and an outside wall.

We were so grateful to long-term friends who organized the complete redecoration of the flat, using their company team. They also went the extra mile and carpeted the entire home at their own expense as a love-gift. That was amazing! The work was done so well that very little serious work had to be done over the fifteen years we lived there, in spite of the hundreds of people who visited the home for a variety of reasons. It was our friendly police sergeant who organized transport and pairs of hands to move us from Marshall Street to Brewer Street. That was such a help, and I don't recall our normally uncompromising traffic wardens slapping on a ticket for parking on a yellow line in a very busy street!

With all this help, the upheaval of moving was reduced to a minimum. Lois had been married toward the end of our time in the Marshall Street Dwellings. Given the lack of local facilities, the Thamesmead church kindly came to the rescue by allowing us to use the church building for the wedding service, while the nearby Community Centre was ideal for the reception. It was a great day.

Reducing our family by one meant that I had the luxury of a study and space to talk with visitors in confidence. All this came at a price of course. The rent of the new flat went up by 80%, and the call to love our neighbour as ourselves rose from nineteen homes to fifty-nine. Living in St James' Residences may have greatly increased our opportunity to meet with fellow tenants but it also cut us off from the rough and tumble of life outside on the streets. That strong metal gate had a lot to do with it— although we would be glad of it in the not too distant future.

New opportunities

It wasn't long before new doors opened for the gospel. With the school on our doorstep, Pam took the opportunity to visit and offer voluntary service. The head was the curate at St James', Piccadilly. Over the next sixteen years Pam enjoyed being in the classroom situation, and increasingly working with small groups of children with reading or behavioural needs. Eventually she made a significant contribution to the challenges facing every city centre school. The children came from a variety of ethnic backgrounds, including those that placed more importance on the sons, and less on the daughters. Being spoilt at home can lead to unacceptable behaviour in the classroom.

The school had a group of notorious characters. Pam had always been good with the young people we had in our home, from our Bexleyheath, New Cross and Thamesmead days. They were always welcome in spite of their misbehaviour and lack of hygiene. She had a quiet authority which meant she never had to raise her voice, just give a clear instruction of what she expected. Behind this authority lay not fear of reprisal or rejection but the relationship she built up with each individual. It was the same in the home. In all the years our four children were living at home, I can't recall a single incident when a family member answered back, or rebelled in any way, openly at least; and our children weren't angels! There are men and women of various nationalities whose prospects were significantly improved because of the work done in those small groups in the primary school.

I don't remember how it came about, but I became deputy leader of the school play-centre. This operated after school, Monday to Friday, during term time. The children arrived at 3.30 pm and were collected by their parents at 6 pm. I committed myself to two sessions a week, on Mondays and Thursdays. Entrusted with keys, it was a simple thing to slip through the gate which provided security between St James' Residences and the school. The play centre gave me an opportunity to draw on my arts and crafts background and encourage such skills lying dormant in the children. We painted portraits of ourselves and each other, we modelled with clay and balsa wood and we spent a term re-creating a small-scale Victorian house, with all its furniture. Over the years, several of the children became really enthusiastic with these sessions. Some of them shone in the subject when going on to their secondary school. Their parents often invited me into their homes when I came across them during my visiting in the area.

Spending valuable time in such small group teaching, or craft activity, meant that most of the boys and girls who filled our church youth activities to capacity over a number of years on a Friday evening came directly from the contact we had with the school in those early years.

A significant opportunity to serve our neighbours stemmed from an approach by our housing officer. The Soho Housing Association had adopted a policy of encouraging the residents of each estate to form a Tenants Association. The idea was to establish a two-way exchange of information and news in the hope that both landlord and tenants could keep each other updated on things like housing policy, rent increases, repairs and problem tenants. I was asked if I would chair the St James' Association. No doubt this was a wonderful opportunity to win the trust of neighbours who may not open their door to normal visiting. However, I was never a lover of church business meetings, let alone a community business meeting, and being a very poor chairman into the bargain, the omens were not good. The prospect of chairing a quarterly meeting of cynical, complaining residents from different cultural backgrounds and languages filled me with horror. Madness must have overtaken me, because I was eventually persuaded to take it on, even though I stayed only long enough to get the thing off the ground.

The first few meetings were generally orderly, give or take the odd rogue rant, and ran along the lines of the agenda. Generally, people are interested only in their personal gripe or contentious issue. However, it wasn't long before open warfare broke out between two elderly Italian women who had been at each other's throats since childhood. In the end, to avoid total confusion, I had to ask them either to stick to the subject on hand or leave the meeting. It worked, because neither came to another meeting, although both continued to speak to me.

Further down the track, the issue of trust raised its head. Who could be trusted with the Association's funds? And, following an end of year party, who could be trusted with the undrunk bottles of wine? We actually had a first-class treasurer in Elizabeth, and the members were happy for her to keep the books, but not the petty cash. The issue was resolved by giving the chairman responsibility for the safe keeping of both the cash and wine.

The new neighbours

Getting to know our neighbours was a priority. At number 27 was Patricia, no longer young, but who still had plenty of style. She claimed to have descended from Russian aristocracy. It was a shame that the glory had faded over the years, not helped by her fondness for alcohol. Patricia managed well with her Home Help. It was as close as she got to having a personal maid in her latter years! There was a period when she needed our help. I made her tea outside of home-help hours, while Pam did the more personal things for her.

One of our last memories was just before she moved to a care home in Whitstable, Kent. Patricia had let us know that she had been invited out to celebrate some special occasion with similarly 'grand' friends. She had taken care to look the part, with hair, makeup and stylish clothing, including a faux leopard skin coat. She left in a taxi. Pam and I were in bed at 10.30 pm and anxious that she hadn't arrived home. Some hours later, Jon woke us to say Patricia was home, but drunk and lying on her door mat, having failed to get the key into the keyhole. Pam suggested that I stay out of the situation as Patricia would be so embarrassed. Pam and Jon helped her up and got her indoors and Pam helped her into bed. Nothing was ever said when we met after that. We visited her in the Whitstable care home when in the area some years later. Patricia was still 'grand' but now sober and very fragile.

Our other immediate neighbour, at number 28, was Tom. He had spent many years on the street before being accommodated in another of Soho's shameful, run-down blocks of flats. When this building passed to the Soho Housing Association, Tom became our neighbour. It took time to win his confidence because at heart he was a loner and his accommodation soon became like the doorway which had once been his home. There was a point when, every few weeks, the entire stairwell was polluted by the most evil smell, just at the time we came home from the Morning Service. We couldn't discover the source of it, except there was a tell-tale stream of green filth that emerged from Tom's home, trailed along the corridor, past our front door, down the stairs, and out into the court yard where it seemed to come to an end. The caretaker insisted that it was a job for our housing officer, who eventually came to check Tom's home. She didn't get a warm welcome, so didn't hang around. Her official report suggested that the cause was the very old 'flower water' Tom had left on a window ledge. No-one was convinced, and the disgusting experience continued.

It was a few weeks later that we caught Tom in the act, dragging a black plastic bag along the corridor, heading for the stairs. The evil green slime was leaving its normal trail. To avoid a scene, I thought it best to let him continue on his journey to the bin-room, while we began disinfecting and cleaning up the foul-smelling mess. When Tom returned, I suggested it was time for us to talk. It wasn't surprising that the explanation had nothing to do with very old flower water. Tom had the same home help as Patrick in the old Dwellings. She insisted on shopping for him, when he really wanted to shop for himself and buy the food he fancied—legs of lamb, pork chops, and sausages—not that he had the facilities to cook them. So, afraid of what his home help would say, he bought the meat and locked it in the original toilet, but never got round to cooking it! Eventually, even Tom couldn't live with the stench, so it had to be dumped—on Sunday mornings, the day the home help didn't call.

Tom died, some years later, in circumstances I didn't remember until I came across my notes used at his funeral. I'm not sure if I volunteered to lead the Service, or if I was asked by Social Services. Or it may even have been Tom who requested it, since, I'm told, he referred to me as 'my friend the reverend'.

The opening comments of my address told a tale...

> Tom was one of a dying breed.
> He insisted on living an independent lifestyle.
> —on the streets, at home, or even when under supervision!
> He didn't take kindly to those who fussed.
> He wasn't impressed by those who thought they knew best.
> He wasn't the easiest person to help at the best of times.
> —illustration: the incident of the rotting meat!
> The Christmas dinner showed a glimpse of another Tom
> —he grunted, 'Thanks mate', with a smallest hint of a smile.
> Tom was a survivor.

He was a 'come-back kid'. Found wandering, with broken
bones, written off but surviving severe chest infections.
But then, only later, giving way to death.

There may have been no family or friends at Tom's funeral, just support workers, but we all felt the poorer for his passing.

As we were moving in, a Bangladeshi family was also moving in upstairs: father, mother and two young children, a boy and girl. I had been out somewhere, but coming home I found our hall full of new divan beds. In the living room, Pam introduced me to a man in his 30s, the husband/father of the family about to move in upstairs. There had been some confusion over keys and he was locked out until the housing officer arrived. Within a couple of hours he had access to his new home and with our help was able to get his bedding upstairs. Over the coming months we developed a good relationship with the family, but only rarely saw the husband around. Eventually, having got to know the wife, Azizun, well, we were told that her husband had been sentenced to a long term in prison. We never discovered what crime had been committed, but ten years later he turned up at the home, causing Azizun to scream from a window for the police to be called.

Immanuel Community Church

If only I could fill these pages with news of crowded congregations, prayer meetings and Bible studies! However, building anything to last involves digging deep trenches in the process of laying a solid foundation. I recently read a book review about the wonderful conversion of a young man caught up in multiple addictions. The reviewer was appreciative of God's life-changing work in him, but complained that, 'two thirds of the book was taken up with grime, leaving only a third to focus on grace.' I appreciate that complaint, but when a new work starts with no-one and nothing, it's not surprising that there is much hard digging to do before, God willing, something solid and lasting appears above ground.

Today, I walk my dogs each morning and afternoons in the Glebe fields still belonging to the parish church. The village of Charlwood is famous for its magnificent oak trees. This autumn has been amazing in terms of the vast numbers of acorns that have fallen, usually about the time of the first frost. One of my favourite trees must have shed many thousands of acorns this year, yet so few take root, become established, and grow into oak trees. Church planting is like that: making it a priority to relate significantly to many people, in the hope that, through the gospel shared by word and life, some will receive the good news of Jesus Christ and be added to both his Church, and the local church.

> One of my favourite trees must have shed many thousands of acorns this year, yet so few take root, become established, and grow into oak trees. Church planting is like that

How many local churches actually come into being, or grow, in this way? A popular preacher, a thriving congregation, and lively worship will often prove attractive to believers who travel from other churches. That church is growing numerically by feeding on other, possibly struggling, churches. This is not church planting. It is simply recycling existing believers.

Thankfully, the events recorded in previous chapters, although often daily experiences, simply punctuated normal life. Looking back at our reporting in the early years, people were being added to the congregation, and some were becoming Christians, needing baptism and a spiritual home. The team, envisaged at the beginning of the Project, began to come together.

Mary O'Neil joined the team in 1985. Having left Thamesmead in 1981 to live in Sandringham Flats, in Charing Cross Road, she was working in the area as a midwife as the Project got under way. Since much of our work was among women, she had an important part to play. Mary was already housed on the edge of Soho, but she successfully obtained a flat in Ingestre Court, the newest of our local tower blocks.

Andrew Murray came to join the team the following year with the support of his church, Bethesda Baptist Church, in Felixstowe. A graduate of Aberdeen University, he was committed to bringing the gospel to city centres. The prospect of being part of a church planting project in Soho was sufficient to attract him away from his work in the Felixstowe docks. It was a marvellous answer to prayer when accommodation in the Marshall Street Dwellings was provided for him. This too may have been in recognition by the Westminster's Housing Department of the work we were doing.

The possibility of forming a church began to impact upon us, not just because additional Christian workers were strengthening our hands, but because we had three new believers seeking baptism. Lois had come to faith before her marriage and we had baptized her at the Thamesmead church, where she now lived and worshipped with her husband, Andrew White.

Immanuel Community Church was formed in Soho on 25 January 1987, with Michael, Pam, Andrew and Mary as founding members. Jon, Margaret and Carol were baptized on February 8th at the Thamesmead church. We received them into membership the following Sunday, at our first communion service.

Andrew and Joy Russell were married and made their home in Soho. This was in the block where Andrew had been living since his arrival. The flat had just one bedroom. Its only advantage was that it was on the second floor, but at the shady back of the building.

Covent Garden and Mayfair

For some time, we had been strengthening our links with the London City Mission, which had been for many years based in Covent Garden. The Mission had workers who witnessed around Piccadilly Circus and we enjoyed fellowship with one of the senior men, Geoff Hollands, and began meeting each week for prayer and Bible study. Geoff acknowledged a weakness in his work, that good work was done door-to-door Monday to Friday, but no-one was around to bring people together on Sundays. He himself lived outside of Central London. Also, he had been invited to set up a City Mission in Derby. Strong churches were ready to support him in the work if he would lead. Out of these discussions came a request that we appoint suitable men to take on the leadership of a new congregation in Covent Garden and attempt some youth work. Geoff gave us a list of contacts who might be willing to form the nucleus of a Sunday congregation. I visited them all. They were mainly elderly but there was the possibility of some attending. But where would we look for leaders?

To quote from a report at the time: 'Brian and Valerie Maidstone, members of the Angel Baptist Church, Clerkenwell, have been set apart by their church to lead this work during its initial stages. Brian's gifts, experience, links with the In-reach Committee from inception, close proximity to both home and work and the full support of Valerie and their son, Jonathan, all point to him being the Lord's gift to the work...' The first Sunday service was held on 1 November 1987. Brian and Val continued to lead this congregation until 1992 when Mike and Gwen Mellor were invited to take up the long-term ministry of the Covent Garden congregation with a view to forming an independent church there.

It was also during this year that we attempted to establish a home group in the neighbouring community of Mayfair. Three women had begun to meet with us on Sunday mornings. They had been members of Westminster Chapel for many years under the ministry of Dr Martyn Lloyd-Jones. After the Doctor's retirement they became unsettled by the new direction taken by his successor. One of the three ladies was Ethel Arnott, who lived

in the Peabody Flats opposite Selfridges, in Oxford Street. Seeing what the Lord was doing in Soho, she began praying that the gospel would also be shared in her community. Eventually, the Soho church members began to hold the monthly afternoon communion in her home, and an occasional Sunday evening fellowship. The main thrust was a twice-monthly group held in Ethel's home on a Wednesday afternoon. I had agreed to spend a morning each week systematically visiting the 400 Peabody flats on the estate.

Although not far from the influential All Souls Church in Langham Place, there was no local church in the immediate area. The Anglican church in Down Street was closed, and a Sunday

The first floor flat in Mayfair where we began meeting in 1988

congregation, made up almost entirely of non-locals, met in St Mark's nearby. Eventually, during this year, between ten and fifteen local people began attending our group. There was no light entertainment provided, apart from a cup of tea and homemade cake! The theme that year was taken from Proverbs, which seemed to hold the interest of the group.

We occasionally invited visiting speakers to join us. These sessions were generally among the most fruitful. I visited the members of the group in their own homes on a regular basis and wondered if this loyal group could become the nucleus of a new church in this significant community.

Chapter 7

The formation of Immanuel Community Church in Soho in 1987, the baptism of three new believers and their reception into church membership, the marriage of Andrew and Joy, the growth of our midweek meeting for prayer and Bible study with up to thirteen attending, the establishing of a new congregation in Covent Garden led by Brian and Val Maidstone, and the twice-monthly group meeting in a Mayfair home, meant that the work was certainly progressing. We added a lunch time meeting in Westminster. I can't recall how the link was made, but we were given free access to the Conference Room in Westminster Social Services, overlooking Berwick Street Market. It was ideally placed with the use of a small kitchen. Around thirty people would arrive between 1pm and 2pm on a Wednesday, once a month. We provided hot drinks with biscuits, and the best programme we could muster. We called the group, 'Lunch and Listen.' The programme was varied, for example:

> Inspector David Strang: The policeman's lot—a happy one?
> Joanna Bogle: National Viewers and Listeners Association.
> Pat Williams: Abortion—convenient or criminal?
> David Blackmore: Keep Sunday Special.
> George Harvey: U Turn Anglia.

Of these, it was the Keep Sunday Special theme which drew the most rewarding guests. Personnel officers from John Lewis and Marks & Spencers came specially to hear the arguments for keeping a day free of trading every week. The reps from these significant traders in Oxford Street asked questions and raised issues and seemed convinced by the answers given from a Biblical and social perspective.

With passing years, it became increasingly difficult to find speakers and themes of this calibre. The support for the meetings gradually became mainly Christian; members from churches in and around London who worked in the area could be counted on to support. For this reason, the themes of 'Lunch and Listen' became more directly Bible-based. Eventually we were to lose the use of this building due to construction work and the meetings closed.

The work ethic for a church planter

1988 was a year of consolidation, when three more members were received: Joy Murray, who was deputy head of Christchurch School, Brick Lane, in the East End; Maggi Graham, who was a ward clerk at the nearby Middlesex Hospital; and Anna Skull, who had come to London from Suffolk to do her nursing training at the Middlesex Hospital. They all contributed very special things to our church life: Joy, with her strong teaching skills and experience; Maggi, the use of her home in Mayfair and outstanding gift of hospitality; and Anna, with her lovely musical gifting.

It was a great luxury to have three full-time members of a team to reach out, engage with the community and respond to invitations to share news of the work among the churches. There was a danger of spending too much time together, discussing policy, sharing news of contacts and simply enjoying fellowship together; however, it was essential for the team to meet regularly, which we did on a Monday morning at 9 am, usually at Mary's home, which was probably the quietest of the three. We allowed ourselves a cup of coffee before working our way through an agenda.

By now we all had separate areas of responsibility and it was important that we knew what each was doing, and how the time was to be spent through the coming week. We were praying usually by 10.15 am. Looking back on the experience of team leadership over two church planting ventures, I'm not sure I had the gifts to cover its many demands. It is, rightly, down to the team leader to set the direction and policy of the project, keep on top of his own ministry and activities yet still having the energy to supervise and encourage other team members. Should there be tensions they too must be resolved fairly, while keeping all members on board. I suspect I didn't always achieve this delicate balance. I have some regrets as I look back.

Given my background, it's no surprise that the work ethic is part and parcel of who I am. I suspect its root lies in my upbringing and lifestyle within my family home. Work dominated almost everything. It was the source of our income and provision for the family. Since our well-being depended on the work being done, day in, day out, my parents just got on with it.

The second influence was the studio where I was employed as a graphic designer and typographer. My working day normally stretched between 9 am and 5.30 pm. What impressed itself on me from the beginning was that someone had to pay for every minute I was there. In fact, the final task of the day was to complete a 'chit' indicating how many hours I had spent designing and for which company. When being set apart for Christian ministry in 1962, I was convinced that the Lord Jesus would expect no less of me in his service. Christian service is not the soft option.

My work ethic became something of a joke among the Soho team and church members, although I can hardly believe it. Apparently, I used to tap my foot when someone was late, kept us waiting, or when I felt time was being wasted. Throughout the Soho years, I maintained a pattern of working every day, Monday to Friday, 8.30 am to 5.30 pm, and each evening until 9 pm. On Monday evenings I relaxed by walking the streets, peering into shop windows, and looking at paintings, mainly in Mayfair.

I kept as much of Saturday free as possible, helping Pam with the family shopping during the morning, then walking around the City, guidebook in hand, in the afternoon. Pam usually preferred to stay at home sewing or knitting. If the weather was particularly nice we would walk through Mayfair, into Hyde Park and head for the Italian Gardens at the top of the Serpentine. We normally took a packed lunch and read books or walked on to the café and enjoyed coffee by the water's edge. Pam was always eager to get home, so we didn't linger. After the evening meal I normally retired to the bathroom, with my sermon notes for the following morning, attempting to get them from the page into my heart while in the bath. Sometimes they ended up in the water! Pam was content with watching 'Casualty'.

Sundays of course, were special. Up early for prayer, and a final check of the sermon notes, breakfast was unhurried. We had access to the Norton Centre from 10 am where we sat round a circular table. Hymn books, Bibles and notes were available. We tried to get these practical jobs done in good time so that we were free to spend time with those coming in to join us. With eleven large windows looking out onto Broadwick Street, it was a good place to be.

Meeting the supporting churches

From the beginning we were aware of the debt we owed to the churches supporting the London In-reach Project. It took time, and a development in affordable printing, to enable us to keep the churches informed regularly by mail, so very quickly at least one evening a week had to be set aside for deputation visiting.

> From the beginning we were aware of the debt we owed to the churches supporting the London In-reach Project

The supporting churches were nation-wide: London, Brighton, Aberystwyth, Ipswich, Hartlepool. Usually driving away from Soho in the early afternoon and often not returning until 3 am the following day. The annual visit to Aberystwyth was the classic. Geoff Thomas was keen to expose his students to the work we were doing. A group of fifty students and church members were assembled in the church hall for a 7.30 pm start. Geoff led the devotions and handed over to me for the remaining hour of slides and commentary. A question and answer session ended with a prayer that the Lord would prosper his work, then a cup of tea before bidding the group farewell and heading back to London.

Aberystwyth was a round trip of 524 miles, always in February, with mountains to negotiate in fog, and often, snow. Arriving back in Soho around 3.30 am, it was essential to find a Residents' parking space, otherwise it would mean getting out before 8 am to be parked legally for the day. An additional challenge arose if I borrowed Jon's car to make the return trip possible from the furthest engagements. He and Jackie were living in Holborn, a twenty-minute walk away from Soho. It was even more difficult to find parking at 3 am there than in the West End, and there was the projector and a case of literature to carry home.

Well over one hundred churches, colleges and Christian Unions requested personal deputation visits through those years, some of them on a yearly basis. On the whole travelling by car was the most reliable means of reaching the destination and getting home again the same evening, which I preferred to save biting into another day and also to save Pam being on her own overnight once Jon was married and living away.

Some visits were frustrating and hair-raising. Winter evenings were generally the church's choice for these visits. There was the regular visit to a church in deepest Essex. One year I arrived in good time by train and was kindly collected at the station by a church member. The meeting went well, the Kodak carousel behaving beautifully—no jammed or spilt slides on this occasion! The same driver dropped me off at the station. It was getting late and he drove away at speed. Climbing a number of stairs to the platform, I kept an eye on the clock. I was in good time. The time the train was due came and went but no train. Walking further along the platform there was a screen saying a train had been trashed earlier that evening and that all services were cancelled for the night. The station was deserted and unstaffed. I was stuck; no mobile phone in those days. I made my way back downstairs to find a handwritten sign which announced that a bus would take London-bound passengers to Upminster, at the very end of the District Line at 11 pm. Hopefully, I could get home. At 1.30 am the next morning, I was climbing the steps of Piccadilly Circus Underground Station, the Kodak Carousel a dead weight, when down the steps poured dozens of devotees of the 'Rocky Horror Show' all dressed for the part. Evidently, they had enjoyed a good evening.

Getting home at a reasonable time wasn't always easy even from the Greater London area. A wonderfully encouraging church in the Croydon area usually arranged for several visits in the course of the year, wanting its various groups to hear the Soho story. This particular evening I arrived late because of a signal problem. The meeting was long anyway, but when I got to the station trains to Victoria were few and far between. Eventually, back in London around 11.30 pm, I thought it was probably worth walking home, via St James' Park. Once again I was lugging the Kodak projector with a case containing literature. Before I got to the footbridge dedicated to Diana, two characters emerged from the shadows of the trees and demanded money. It was the last straw. I'd had enough for one day, now this. I put the projector and my case on the ground, telling them I was tired and on my way home. I couldn't be bothered to argue the point. I put my hand in the pocket which held a handful of loose change, the remains of the train fare, and handed it over. Then I ignored them, picked up the Kodak and case and continued over the bridge and home.

The wrong chauffeur!

On two occasions I faced problems of another kind. Preaching at a church in Colchester one Sunday, I arrived at the station and searched the faces of people waiting to meet and greet the passengers. No-one recognized me apparently. I went out to the car park and stood waiting. Within two or three minutes a small white car arrived. A man in his seventies stepped out, shook me warmly by the hand and opened the passenger door for me to sit with him in the front. He said we had time for coffee at home before heading for the service. Good, I fancied that. Once home, the coffee was all ready and served with a biscuit by the lady of the house. It was only when they began to question me about people they knew (but I didn't) and places where missionary work was being done (that I had never heard of) it dawned on me that they had picked up the wrong preacher! The woman panicked, took the half-drunk cup of coffee out of my hand and ushered me back into the car. As we drove into the station car park an Asian man stood, waiting. In a moment, they were all over him—leaving me to wonder what would happen now. Had my driver been and gone again? Thankfully, the car arrived ten minutes later. The vestry team and congregation saw the amusing side and made the most of it throughout the day—at my expense.

Something similar happened when arriving for a deputation meeting in Dorchester. Once again, I had travelled by train (our car had been stolen on New Year's Day), and I stood in the car park, wondering who was going to collect me. To my amazement the door of a large car opened and a chauffeur strode towards me. 'Good evening, sir' he said, taking my case of literature and opening a back door of the car. I got in, although thinking it all very odd; but then, the church was led by an American couple and perhaps they treated all their guest speakers like this? 'Hold it.' I called to the chauffeur, 'I think you have the wrong man!' 'Aren't you the member of the Gas Board?' he asked. He was not amused when I introduced myself. The car was brought to a rapid halt, the back door opened, the case was thrust into my hand and the car reversed at speed back into the car park. He didn't even wish me well with the deputation meeting. A more modest car arrived later to collect me.

In sharp contrast, I made my way by train to a reputable church near Bath. I admired the minister tremendously, an unrivalled historian among the Particular Baptist churches. The meeting was warm and enthusiastic and was followed by probing questions. Time was passing. I needn't have worried. One of the young men explained that he travelled all over the country with his job, and, for him, London was just down the road. He would drive me home, and he did! Arriving in Marshall Street well after midnight, we slipped indoors quietly, to share a cup of coffee before he began his return journey. That's the best of Christians for you!

When I look down the long list of meetings today, I feel weary. I get flashbacks of joy, encouragement and pain when I think of the variety of experiences among so many groups. To do one of these meetings once a week was normal, and sometimes, under pressure, it meant travelling and speaking twice or three times a week. Churches want you when they want you, not always when it is convenient for you. Yet, some of the individuals met on these occasions became close personal friends who have continued in touch into retirement years.

Only the Lord knows what the prayers and sacrificial giving of these supporters achieved over the years. Like the apostle, I thank God for them, and pray with joy because of their partnership in the gospel from the day the project began.

Growing on

1989 held further encouragements for us. Two new believers were baptized and received into membership. Virginia lived opposite us in St James' Residences, with her two young children, Zenaida and Daniel, who was a strong Liverpool supporter. With family in the Philippines, Virginia came to live in London having married a man from Soho's Italian community. Always with a ready smile, Virginia's circumstances and security had been changed beyond recognition by the illness and early death of her husband. Mary O'Neil was well equipped for providing the support Virginia and the family needed in these circumstances. The outcome was that God graciously met with the family at this time of grief, leading Virginia to a personal faith in Jesus Christ. The church encouraged her to begin her life of discipleship by obeying her Lord in believer's baptism. Needing to down-size, the family moved to a more suitable flat in Wardour Street, still in the heart of our catchment area. By now the church was meeting informally on Sunday evenings, using homes in Mayfair and Soho. Virginia willingly hosted one of these, which helped us to keep her involved in the fellowship of the church family.

David joined the Sunday morning service through a friendship made with one of our members on a Christian holiday. Employed in the internet industry he would have been a help if we had our own buildings to equip. David needed basic teaching and a solid foundation for his life. He experienced the sadness of losing his father when he chose to leave the family home when David was eight years old. The experience damaged him into adulthood. To some extent, the church family provided much of what David had been missing. Sunday and one-to-one ministry eventually brought him to faith, baptism and membership of the church.

Chapter 9

Youth and literature

In 1988 we had received permission to base two youth groups in the Marshall Street Leisure Centre. Dated and in need of thorough renovation, there was a large child-proof room available on an upper floor. On 11 January 1989, we launched two youth groups for 5–10 and 11–16 year-olds over a three-hour period on Friday evenings. We were blessed with the regulation number and mix of male/female youth leaders, and as many children as we needed to make this work worthwhile.

Youth work became something of an institution in the community, appreciated by parents coping with children in cramped homes and by the Soho Society who recognized the need but who were ill-equipped to do anything themselves. They did offer to pass on an outdated record player, the sum-total of the equipment they had available.

Looking back, the boys' group, particularly, was pretty non-PC! Government guidelines for groups like ours began to force change on some of our activities in the 1990s, but for the present we had a free hand. We always aimed to have three adult leaders present for the twenty members. Given our ethnic mix, it was important to lay down firm rules covering respect for the leaders, and each other, regular attendance (or your place is offered to someone on the waiting list), no bad language, and no bullying. Suspension was a real option in the event of failure. Given this was a church organization, each member was expected to respect the Bible time and prayer which ended each session.

Later, incoming Government Guidelines robbed the lads of their favourite game: British Bulldog! Living in small accommodation without gardens and attending a school with a play area no bigger than a small yard, the boys had energy to spare. The game involved all the boys grouping at one end of the long hall, waiting for the shout, 'British Bulldog.' The idea was for the lads to make a dash to the safety of the other end, while the three leaders waited to pounce, grabbing any of the youngsters and lifting them off the ground, at which point they were 'out'. The noise was horrendous, the fun enormous! The new guidelines ruled the game too rough and dangerous for the poor boys and it also involved leaders man-handling the boys. Now, children must not be touched. Thankfully we were at least left with football which was played enthusiastically and soaked up some of the energy.

By Christmas 1988 we were fully equipped and able to produce our own literature to a high level. Unbelievably, we were by then the proud owners of an Apple Mac and an Epson Office Printer. This was all due to a series of visits to Emmanuel, Northwood. Richard Bewes had been the vicar, leaving to take over from Dr John Stott at All Souls, Langham Place, so the ground had been prepared. Many of the members had caught the vision of the gospel in Central London, and visits were warmly welcoming and well supported. Emmanuel was a missionary church in terms of outlook, sending, and supporting gospel work in Africa particularly. Our meetings took place in the 'Africa Room'.

For many years Emmanuel had held a well-publicized auction of quality furniture and other goods, raising thousands of pounds for Christian work overseas each year. In 1987 we were approached about receiving a gift from the auction to help our work. The ability to produce and print our own publicity was a pressing need for us, which also appealed to our good friends at Emmanuel. The cost of the equipment was £4000—and that was the amount given. We were truly thankful and told them so.

So, as Christmas 1988 approached we were prepared.

900 Carol Service Invitations, designed, folded and delivered to local homes.

5,000 tracts written, printed, folded and placed behind car windscreen wipers over the Christmas / New Year period.

350 Christmas cards designed, enveloped, addressed and delivered to our closest contacts.

Gifts for the lonely and housebound, wrapped, labelled and delivered. 500 New Year motto texts printed for church members and congregation and mailed to supporters.

A special edition of our *inContact* news update, written, folded by hand, enveloped, addressed, and mailed to over 400 supporting churches and groups.

The London In-reach Project had been launched seven years earlier. There was much to challenge, but a great deal more to praise the Lord for.

We were not confident in ourselves nor were we strong, but we knew Someone who was! Our motto text for this busy period was, 'The LORD bless you and keep you; the LORD make his face shine upon you, and be gracious to you, the

We were not confident in ourselves nor were we strong, but we knew Someone who was!

LORD turn his face toward you and give you peace' (Numbers 6:24–25).

Andrew Murray had been part of the team since 1986. He had arrived with the approval of his home church in Felixstowe, Suffolk. Over the past four years we had watched him grow in maturity and his ability to grasp the essentials of city centre evangelism. He also displayed a gift for leading the congregation in worship, teaching the Bible and resolving complicated pastoral issues. Having Joy as his wife was an additional asset. The whole church recognized God's gracious gift to us at a communion service in 1990 when Andrew was formally set aside as an Elder with us.

Paul began to worship with us this year. His family home was in Coventry. He was a trained chef and arrived in the West End to take up an appointment in a five-star hotel in Piccadilly. He found central London overwhelming. At that time there was an evangelical group working to make contact with people, like Paul, from out of London, needing to link with Christians who could guide and support them through all the confusion of the London scene. Well designed information cards were displayed on the tables in cafés, burger bars around the main line stations and anywhere else that new arrivals might gather.

Paul gave me a ring and we arranged to meet in Grosvenor Square at 2 pm that afternoon. No sooner had we begun to share areas of Paul's background when black clouds dumped an enormous rain storm on us. We ran into a small, Italian coffee shop, just off the Square, finding space among the regulars. Coffee was ordered and a couple of currant buns, mainly to justify the time and space we were likely to need sheltering and talking. Paul continued to share his past experience at length, while I responded with assurances of the support and encouragement both I and the church would give him. When it was time for Paul to check in at the hotel, I agreed to walk with him. There was just the bill to pay for the coffees and buns consumed. Heading for the till it dawned on me I hadn't come prepared. Did I have any money on me at all? It was while I was rummaging around in my pockets, that the man behind the counter said that someone had already paid for what we owed. He had been listening to our conversation in the cramped conditions, was impressed with what he heard, and felt he wanted to show his appreciation by settling the bill in full. I was encouraged to continue believing in angels! Paul became a church member, attending and supporting in every way possible that his shift working allowed.

A fresh start

Eight years passed, making a deep dent in the promise Pam and I made to give ten years to planting the church in Soho. A possible major change in leadership within the next two years would involve much prayer, open discussion within the church, and seeking the advice of those who had followed us so closely over these early years. Most churches find that replacement of leadership can take months—or even years. The Project to plant a church in Soho had received more than its fair share of publicity from the beginning. The work had featured in the evangelical press and it even drew the attention of the journal of the Westminster Seminary in the USA.

The issue of leadership continued to occupy our minds, but did it need to be an immediate issue for us? Was a radical change of leadership essential at this point? Eventually, the church agreed to invite me to continue serving as pastor beyond the ten-year agreement, until retirement, in 2001.

Neither Pam nor I presumed such an invitation would be given, and we took time to assess ourselves as well as the needs of the church. Were our gifts and style of working still relevant? Were our relationships good and solid within the membership? Were we both in sufficient health to continue in the leadership role?

When looking at ourselves, and our remaining years of service, we could not identify any other church or area of work where we could happily settle and use our remaining time. Soho was in our blood, and the church the Lord had brought together was in our heart. Our response to the church's kind invitation was a heart-felt, 'Yes, please. Thank you.'

It wasn't a condition of our responding positively, but we asked if it would be possible to take a three-month sabbatical before embarking on the next lap. With almost thirty years of ministry behind us, usually concluding one ministry one Sunday, moving house, and beginning the new ministry on the following Sunday, it would be good to step back for this period. This was readily agreed. The sabbatical was spent catching up with neglected family members and friends. Pam supported a school journey to Sayer's Croft and spent an extended time with our daughters and grandchildren. I had the privilege of enjoying three weeks in Israel, ten days as part of a tour with a son-in-law, the remainder wandering alone around the relatively safe city of Jerusalem.

At some point, I was presented with the following covenant statement:

'We, the people of Immanuel Community Church, give thanks to the Lord for blessing us with your ministry.

We recognise the gifts that the Lord has given you and we therefore set you apart to minister his word to us and to provide the pastoral care we need.

We pledge our love and our submission to your God-given authority, we commit ourselves to provide for your material support, and we promise to keep you faithfully in our prayers.'

Easter Day, 1990

The rest and change of a sabbatical was refreshing, but long enough to make me impatient to get back and begin work on the next stage of growing the planted church in Soho.

Like all living and growing things, the church needed variety and an increasing quality in the care and feeding it was receiving. Sunday morning was the obvious time to meet the needs of the local members of the congregation. The teaching plan tended to reflect the fact that we had a 'seasonal' congregation and membership. Students, nurses, teachers, trainee doctors, etc were missing for several weeks in the year. Others enjoyed summer holidays and time away from the heat of Central London, regularly reducing our numbers to a third.

> Like all living and growing things, the church needed variety and an increasing quality in the care and feeding it was receiving

This meant planning for themes to fit into a three-month cycle. We developed mini themes to run while numbers were low and attempted to balance themes from the Old and New Testaments, usually finding ways of linking with whatever knowledge our locals had of these passages.

Two approaches to our peculiar situation seemed to enhance our opportunities to make good use of these 'down' Sundays. The first was the Christmas period, which involved low numbers for around four or five weeks, although our afternoon Carol Services were well supported with eighty attending the final Carol Service in the Norton Centre. All preachers need a new infusion of insight into the wonder and mystery of the incarnation of Jesus to save the celebration of Christmas from the traditional round. We planned an 'Isaiah' Christmas, followed by a Matthew, Mark, Luke and a John Christmas in successive years. All readings, carols and talk themes would be drawn mainly from the designated book. This not only spared the leader from the frantic search for yet another view of a familiar passage, but the theme could be drawn out over the entire advent period.

Our summer Sunday

Early on in our life together as a church, having discovered how reduced the morning congregation could be during the summer weeks, we devised a radical change in the programme. Why shouldn't those left behind in London also enjoy a change—a relaxed fellowship and the opportunity to experience something different? Those still in Soho arrived at 10.30 am to a warm welcome and thirty minutes of praise and prayer. At 11 am they were invited to enjoy delicious Italian bread, butter, cheese or marmalade. Tea, coffee and cold drinks were also served. People were encouraged to mix and get to know each other during this time. By 11.30 am the refreshments were over and everything cleared away. At 11.40 am we were back in our seats for a Bible reading, prayer and a twenty minute, straight-to-the-point Bible talk.

The congregation soon adapted to the plan: those able to stay for the afternoon brought their own lunch, plus an extra to share. Berkeley Square was our favourite venue, but there was plenty of choice. Lunch and much chatting and relaxation in the sunshine over, there was a gentle

A fresh start

route to follow, introducing us to some historic area, building, or place of Christian interest. We walked by the Thames at every opportunity. By 3.30 pm we had reached our destination, and received an outline talk on the importance of where we were. A prayer, farewell, and we were heading for home by 4 pm.

Our destination may have been St Mary Woolnoth, in the City, where John Newton preached powerfully from 1780 until his death in 1807. Or it might have been Bunhill Fields, City Road, where 123,000 Protestants are buried, including those of the poet William Blake, Baptists like John Bunyan, Joseph Hart and John Rippon, the pamphleteer and novelist Daniel Defoe, great theologians like Thomas Goodwin and John Owen, the hymn writer Isaac Watts, John Wesley's mother Susanna and many more. We would certainly include St Paul's Yard where copies of Tyndale's New Testament were publicly burnt on 27 October 1526.

Smithfield Market was also on our itinerary. Here, men and women were burned for holding the Protestant faith. Almost three hundred believers were martyred during the reign of Mary Tudor, between forty-five and fifty of them dying here, including John Rogers, John Bradford and John Philpot.

Another favourite route followed the course of the Tyburn River, through Mayfair to Marble Arch, where at the junction of Edgware Road and Bayswater Road a circular stone engraved 'The Site of Tyburn Tree' marked the site where twenty-four condemned prisoners could be hanged at the same time, on a triangular frame. Tyburn was first used as a place of execution in 1177 and was in regular use for six hundred years. An estimated 50,000 executions took place until 1783. Those condemned for anything from murder to cattle stealing were imprisoned at New Gate Prison before being taken in open carts along Oxford Street, to the jeers of multitudes. Following the Reformation, one hundred and five Catholics were executed here as heretics. They are remembered in a nearby Convent, apparently with relics of the deceased on display!

No imagination is needed to capture the enjoyment of walking, talking and learning together on these (usually) lovely summer afternoons. These relaxed Sundays did much to hold us together and bridge the gap until the church family was complete again. Those who preferred a more traditional

Sunday evening could visit the churches at the Angel or Highbury if they preferred.

More challenging was my suggestion that, as a new church and since we spent so much time together, we could use the occasional fifth Sunday evening in a month to visit other central London churches to share their worship, and to experience what it was about the preaching that drew such large congregations, for the most part from outside London. The possibilities included a wide spectrum of church life: All Souls at Langham Place, just a short stroll away; St Helen's, Bishopsgate in the City; the Metropolitan Tabernacle at Elephant and Castle; and even Holy Trinity in Brompton Road.

One summer afternoon, we were caught in a torrential downpour and ended up in the congregation of Westminster Abbey. The service was reverent, and the sermon was well constructed, relevant and free of obvious error. The congregation was rather poor. It's not a bad thing to experience what goes on in our great national institutions, although none of us would probably volunteer to go again.

One Easter Sunday afternoon we were at the end of our local programme, having begun with praise in St James' Park at 7 am, and I was eager to hear some strong resurrection preaching. I walked to St Paul's Cathedral and joined a congregation of around five hundred people for Evensong. The seating had been turned around to face the great main doors. Rocks had been piled high and topped by a large rugged cross. There were no responsive readings or choir pieces, just a series of carefully chosen resurrection readings punctuated by several classic Easter hymns. The preacher was Michael Saward, one of the resident clergy. The sermon was pure gospel—biblical and heart-warming, challenging and appealing, and preached with conviction and power. My heart was still singing as I walked home along the Strand.

Pam would usually join me on the occasions I felt St Helen's was the place to be. We would find ourselves sitting among students, hundreds of them, young men, dressed down with uncombed hair, unshaven chins, but relaxed and welcoming. The music was contemporary but easy to take on board. There was just a nod to the Prayer Book as faith was confessed. Dick Lucas wasn't usually around, but David Jackman, Hugh Palmer or another team member would teach clearly, and apply the message effectively.

All Souls tended to have a broader-based congregation and had more of a family feel. The congregation filled the main building, with an overflow provided for downstairs. Everything was wonderfully efficient: the welcome and the paperwork needed to steer us through the service was offered with a smile. Clergy members and others led the service, reading the Bible and prayers with clarity. The orchestra led the singing, encouraging us to sing out in a way that it is not possible, for some reason, in a small congregation. As much as I admired the church and enjoyed my occasional visits, it was a challenging fact that at the end of the day the mighty congregation would disperse and make little if any impact on the nearby community of Soho! This was a reason for us to be there, with a mission for us to fulfil by living and sharing Christ with those who lived in that community.

Once or twice I spent an evening with the internationally known Holy Trinity, Brompton. No-one fancied joining me as far as I remember. There might even have been some raised eyebrows at my going. The home and power base of the internationally used Alpha Course, HTB specialized in informal services and attracted many hundreds of young people to its varied activities. The building (near Harrods) was buzzing with groups chatting and laughing. I was there with time to spare but ended up having to sit near the back. At the time, the worship music group was trend-setting, led by a strong female soloist and backed up with guitars and drums. The first thirty or forty minutes was largely taken up with song singing, much of it repetitive. Toward the end, even young worshippers were sagging, and sitting down to take a break! The service leader welcomed us and introduced a large group of visitors from a church in Scandinavia. Then a Bible reading, a prayer, followed by a forty-minute sermon, given in the then novel 'walk-about' style. It was Bible-based and completely relevant, given the professional types making up the congregation. There were no prophecies, or speaking in tongues, just enthusiastic worship, and a challenge to live out the teaching given in Paul's letter to Timothy. I went into the service and left it without anyone saying a single word to me!

One winter's evening, Pam and I crossed the Thames and joined the large crowd entering Spurgeon's Tabernacle. The historic building was full, including the gallery. Many in the congregation were young, foreign students. The minister, Dr Peter Masters, had built a solid base for independent, reformed evangelical baptist ministry over many years. It was like stepping back into the 1950s with the King James' Bible being the version of choice, and the extensive hymn book of their own making. We recognized at least some members of the congregation who had travelled from North London to be there. The preaching was strong, Biblical, and directed against modern trends among the churches. The Tabernacle seemed to be a bastion against those movements which were attempting to make worship and preaching relevant to our age. It felt like a safe haven for those believers anxious to hold on to the language and style of worship of a past generation.

I found these occasional visits instructive and endlessly fascinating. In part, this flowed from the fact that I was just a visitor, and not responsible for what went on. Other people bore responsibility for welcoming, contributing to the Service, not to mention the preaching, and theirs was the disappointment when people just didn't turn up!

Each of the churches visited was crowded and flourishing numerically. They each had a personality of their own and attracted people whose needs were being met there. Yet on none of these occasions did I return home with a heavy heart, feeling that the Soho congregation was small and insignificant. I felt rather that our infant church had the potential to be cutting edge, and capable of doing a unique and essential work beyond the scope of those large gathered congregations. Their congregations largely travelled in from outside London or at least well away from the building, while our small congregation lived among the people in Soho and Mayfair throughout the week.

Their congregations largely travelled in from outside London or at least well away from the building, while our small congregation lived among the people in Soho and Mayfair throughout the week

Towards a normal church

The concept of a team being involved in church planting runs parallel with the expansion of the early church in Acts, from Jerusalem to Antioch. It was there that Paul, Barnabas and John Mark were sent out by the church to preach the gospel in Cyprus and mainland Asia minor, now Turkey!

Mary O'Neil had joined Pam and me in 1985, and Andrew Murray came to strengthen our hands by joining us the following year. There was steady progress, with believers being baptized and joining the church through each year. Towards the end of 1988, we were reporting progress at the sixth Annual Meeting of the London In-reach Project. The membership now stood at ten and the congregation numbered thirty, including four Roman Catholics. Eleven of us were committed to supporting the weekly prayer and Bible study.

I was able to share that the members had begun meeting monthly, on a Sunday afternoon, to remember the Lord Jesus in sharing communion together, with prayer and praise, then enjoying a relaxed fellowship meal together. It was one of the rare occasions when unbelievers were not present.

Mary O'Neil returned to Soho about this time from a three-month period of convalescence, following surgery. Having returned it seemed to her that much was the same, little spiritual movement in the lives of her contacts, and the Sunday Services showing no noticeable numerical growth. She also estimated that twenty-five contacts had died in a single block of flats over the past six years, in addition to those who had moved out of the area.

Andrew pointed out in his report that it was now a year since his marriage to Joy. In addition to his marriage responsibilities, he had taken on a new flat and a new job, and was finding that it was taking time to get used to the change. The Project Committee had released him from the work, to study four days each week at home, and it wasn't easy balancing the demands on his time. The course, directed by the late Bob Sheehan, was designed to cover both Old and New Testaments in two years, with church history and some theology also included.

Our income for 1989 was £18,500, and our expenditure was £18,000. So our needs were wonderfully met for another year—just.

During the following year, 1990, it was felt that it was time to begin running the team down. This had always been the policy in planting a church in Soho, following the New Testament pattern: a baptized membership, with elders and deacons appointed, and every member a gifted minister of the church. The team had the privilege of concentrating on the task full time over a number of years. Mary had served for five years, and Andrew three and a half years. It was shake-out time. There is a point in initiating new work when a team is no longer justified. I would take my turn in due time. Mary applied to the London City Mission, and was accepted as a trainee missionary, transferring her membership to Highbury Baptist Church. Andrew was appointed secretary to Soho Parish School.

The running down of the team was a major step to take, but it enabled us to become a more 'normal' church, without the special advantages enjoyed during the initial years. 1990 was a significant year. My role was now more clearly defined: to pastor the growing church, attempt to provide the right diet on Sundays (morning and evening) whilst attempting deeper studies, with prayer, during the mid-week meeting. Systematic visiting must continue on a weekly basis in an ever-changing community. It was a challenge to find the time and energy to re-visit existing contacts, while still making new contacts in the more obscure areas. Having covered the main housing blocks, I began visiting every building which might contain accommodation. This included stairways where brothels, photographic studios, hairdressers, and massage parlours shared space with those living on site.

Jackie Reece and Nicola Foulds were received into membership in 1991. Jackie had been a member of a north London church, but was now living in nearby Lamb's Conduit Street. She was on the staff of the Marks and Spencer store in Oxford Street. Nicola was a law student and had set her sights on becoming a barrister. When first coming to London, she had joined the crowds of students attending All Souls but found it too big, lacking the personal touch. With young people, students of her own age in membership and with great hospitality available all day on Sundays, she settled happily into the Soho scene.

Covent Garden

In 1992, the Project Committee took the step of appointing Mike Mellor as full-time leader of the work in Covent Garden. Brian and Val Maidstone had maintained a Sunday service and a fortnightly Tuesday evening Bible study, over the past five years. Thirty local people had dropped in during that time. The Sunday congregation averaged twelve, with seven attending the mid-week study. It had proved hard to build up the numbers in spite of London City Mission workers visiting regularly in the area. It was considered to be an advantage in appointing full-time workers who would visit the homes, as well as lead the Sunday activities.

Mike and Gwen were received into the membership of 'Immanuel.' This was always going to be a temporary arrangement, though a Biblical one. With some years of pastoral and evangelistic experience behind them they would develop their own approach and policies for the work in a very different community. Mike and I set aside time on Tuesday lunchtimes, to share and pray together.

Mike and Gwen came with their own backing and prayer support. Funds were raised to provide a family home in Stukely Street, in the heart of Covent Garden. Their Sunday Services and activities developed encouragingly, Mike's warm ministry and personality proving attractive to a wide variety of locals and students. The renovated London City Mission Centre, with café, was an attractive place in which to base the work. Gwen grasped a local opportunity, and established a well-supported pre-school group.

Gradually, independence from the Soho church was desirable and possible. Attempts were made to link the two congregations occasionally on a Sunday afternoon, to share things of value to both, but it never really worked. In hindsight this is not surprising. We were each reaching people in our own communities, and Soho and Covent Garden locals had little in common. Central London is not a large, noisy, spread, but a collection of small villages, living cheek by jowl, separated by major road routes. Each has its own origin, history, life-style and pride. Had it been possible to plant a church in Mayfair, that too would have been unique. The work of the gospel was expanding.

Around 1992, the congregation outside the Charles Norton Centre on Broadwick Street where we worshipped for 10 years.

Through discouragement

The Lord had been so good to us since our arrival in Soho ten years earlier. It was now 1993 and a church had been established after a slow beginning. Sixteen believers were now in membership, seven joining us after baptism. A congregation of about thirty swelled our numbers on Sunday mornings in the Charles Norton Centre. As the year began, we had no inkling of the changes and challenges which were to confront us.

Having chosen Isaiah 55:12 as our motto for the year: 'You will go out in joy, and be led forth in peace', we hoped for a year of growth in every area. Instead we were hammered. The first blow concerned our Sunday base, the

Charles Norton Centre. Age Concern were needing to reduce their costs by continuing to work in Covent Garden only. This might possibly leave the Soho building available for us. There was talk of the possibility of our taking up the lease for around £10,000 per annum—an amazing bargain given that, at that time, only Tokyo and New York were more expensive than London per square foot. Our income allowed nothing by way of reserves—but we had a great God! It was a time to trust and pray. We did that, earnestly. A time was set when an offer would have to be made.

The previous Sunday morning, our preaching theme had brought us to Joshua chapter 3, the crossing of Jordan after the long wilderness years. Having arrived at the Jordan, the Israelites camped for three days. The crossing was to be orderly. The nation would be led by the ark, carried by the priestly Levites. The tribes would follow in order, leaving a gap of a thousand yards. Their task was to follow: 'Then you will know which way to go…' The Lord promised Joshua that he would be exalted in the eyes of the people, and they would know that the Lord was with him just as he had been with Moses. The forward move began, the priests having been instructed to walk in, and stand, in the water of the Jordan. Joshua assured them that, having done that, the down-stream flow would be 'cut off and stand up in a heap.' They faced a trial of their faith and obedience; it was the harvest season, and the Jordan was in full flood. However, as soon as the priests' feet were in the water, the flow stopped and both they and the tribes crossed the Jordan on dry ground.

Surely this was a God-sent message for us? The incident contains precious assurance and promises: 'I will exalt you', 'I am with you', 'You will know that the living God is among you.' Exactly what we needed to hear in the circumstances.

The following day, Monday, was the deadline. There was much prayer and excitement to see what the Lord would do. The day was spent waiting, expecting the Lord to clear the barrier to our going forward, enabling us to continue and progress in his work. The daily post came and went. Just circulars, but no miraculous gift. 8 pm arrived, the set time to remove our Bibles and hymn books from the Centre and to hand back the keys. Andrew and I shared the task of emptying cupboards, leaving everything tidy. We worked in silence, wondering what the Lord was doing with us.

The only alternative was to request the use of the Parish School, in Great Windmill Street. There had been a change of Headteacher and Derek Holbird, a warm and helpful Christian, made it possible for us to use the main hall each Sunday. Several of us were active in the School during the week which probably made the offer possible.

I suppose most of us normally expect any radical disappointment or loss the Lord brings to result in some benefit not realised in the confusion of trial. True, we had space to accommodate the congregation, but it was less than ideal, and proved to be the cause of losing a number of long-term members of the congregation. The School itself was a Victorian building, tall and cramped on a small site. The main space was the hall, thirty-two steps up from the ground floor. Elderly members of the congregation, used to arriving at the Centre below their flat by the lift, had no appetite to travel several hundred yards. It wasn't just the distance, our new base was situated in an unattractive area. In the early 1990s, Great Windmill Street was significantly involved in the sex industry. Brothels and clubs actually existed either side of the School gate, and opposite it. The famous Windmill

The church members in 1995

Theatre was a little further down the street. We had no alternative but to accept Derek Holbird's kind offer with thanks, and press on, hoping to build again.

But there was more. I still have our church Diary for March 1997. It is smoke-stained and blotched with soot. A fire destroyed the bedroom of Ethel Arnott's Mayfair home around this time. She had switched on an electric fire before going to bed and drawn the curtains before leaving the room. A draught blew the curtains across the fire, and they caught alight. Her alarm soon brought help, but it was impossible for her to continue living there. She saw it as an opportunity to go into Care. This brought to an end our hopes of establishing a Mayfair congregation. The venue for two of our meetings was no longer available to us. Ethel had pasted an old print to the back of her smoke-stained Diary, entitled:

TRUST THE LORD
Lord I would trust the past to the mercy of God
the present to His love
the future to His providence
St Augustine

Despite these serious discouragements, evangelistic opportunities were flowing. Money was in hand to buy advertising space in the Piccadilly Underground. The design was bold and the text strong. A professional finish was required. We booked eight sites on the up escalator. A solid black background, with a symbolized stable in white, stood out well. The wording was equally stark and strong:

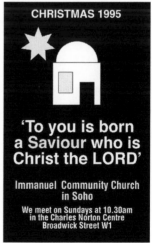

CHRISTMAS 1995

'To you is born a Saviour who is Christ the LORD'

Immanuel Community Church in Soho

We meet on Sundays at 10.30am in the Charles Norton Centre Broadwick Street W1

CHRISTMAS 1995
To you is born a Saviour who is
Christ the LORD
IMMANUEL COMMUNITY CHURCH
in SOHO

In 1995 we bought eight sites on the up-escalator at Piccadilly

With twenty-three trains running every hour, we estimated that these may have caught the eye of some 25,000 people each day over a ten-day period. It was disappointing that, a few days later, someone stuck circular stickers over the word, 'Saviour'. Unbelief was striking back. Later, encouraged by specific gifts given for the purpose, we rented three large sites on the main platform. The black had served us well, combined with yellow, so we repeated it. This time, we featured a Child lying in a Manger, with the message:

SILENT MIGHT
The Saviour of the World!
IMMANUEL COMMUNITY CHURCH IN SOHO

This time, the posters all survived unspoiled, but this was the last opportunity we had—the really big commercial companies began to buy up every available space from that year on!

Another blow struck during 1996. The Social Services room, the venue for 'Lunch and Listen', or 'Commercial Break' as it was now known, was no longer available to us. Its demolition was to be part of the redevelopment of the Berwick Market area. Since we had no alternative meeting space, the group was closed. Thankfully, there were four tremendous encouragements awaiting us later in the year.

Encouragement

It was a Christmas Day service, in the School Hall. Numbers were small due to the usual seasonal scattering. We sat in a circle, feeling a bit exposed in the large space. It was almost time to begin when the door opened, and in walked a ready-made family: father, mother and two little girls, Jessica and Lucy. Later, Holly was born while our friends were still with us. I never discovered how they found us but we made them welcome.

Nigel and Julia lived in the part of St James' Palace called 'The Ewer'. Nigel worked as a restorer of the Royal antique furniture. They, like Ethel Arnott and her friends, had been members of Westminster Chapel. Nigel and Julia were warm and mature Christians who were able to contribute to the life of our church. They became members with us in 1996. Their children added to the growing number of small children belonging to church family members. Joy and Andrew had already been building their family: Asha, John and Abi arriving, nicely spaced, over recent years. Jon and Jackie had married in 1994, one of two marriages between members, and they had Hannah and Chloe. We never lacked women to supervise the crèche; Maggi Graham especially, was ready-made for the task, and in her element when surrounded by the little ones.

Alisdair Gould also came into membership with us that year. He had known about the Soho church when in membership with a supporting Suffolk Church. He was a teacher, specializing in working with special needs children. He was single, and quite a character. Amazingly, we were able to accommodate him in Andrew and Joy's old home in the Marshall Street Dwellings. His introduction to Soho was less than ideal. Walking to the Service one Sunday morning, the streets empty, he was approached by two men who demanded money. Having none, he was frogmarched to the nearest cashpoint and persuaded to draw out some cash. Thankfully, he hadn't been paid, so they had to be content with £20—the sum total of his wealth at the time. On another occasion, going into a telephone kiosk he emptied his pocket of change and left it lying on the shelf ready to put more coins in should he need them. Suddenly, a young man snatched open the door, grabbed the money and was gone before Alisdair realised what was happening. He soon learned to live on his wits during his Soho years!

The discouragement of 1993 and the loss of Charles Norton Centre was amazingly offset sometime later when, within months of each other, two envelopes arrived containing gifts which were capable of really providing for church needs. I was entrusted with the names and address of the gracious givers but promised to treat them as anonymous. In one gift card was a cheque for £60,000. This blew us away! Having written to thank these supporters sincerely, and assured them that we would regard this gift as the provision of the Lord himself, a warm friendship developed. Apparently, the Lord had prospered the family business, and the gift was their thanksgiving to him. Some months passed and the family was still being kept aware of our thinking on how the gift could best be used. Then, another greeting arrived, with a cheque for £200,000! By now we were convinced that such provision should be used for a permanent meeting place, providing for our need of space for services, a study and prayer area, an office, and a kitchen to provide for hospitality needs.

An elaborate specification for what we had in mind was prepared, laying out our needs in detail. When we were satisfied, we listed every Agent involved in buying and selling in Soho, and delivered our requirements to the office of each in person. Surely, £260,000 would result in some response. We waited and prayed. Nothing! When checking with a leading Agent that he had received our request, I was told to approach them again when we had £500,000 to spend. We never did.

Family accommodation was the second obvious need. The Soho church, with its outreach ministry, could never survive if its leaders were forced to move out of the community. It was Carol Conner who introduced us to a friend who was wanting to move from her flat. She lived in a large three-bedroomed flat on the 16th floor of Kemp House, in Berwick Street. Apparently, mortgages are not usually given on accommodation over a particular height, but we didn't need a mortgage. We arranged for the usual searches and surveys. The accommodation was clearly God-given. This was a city-centre family home, with generous space. It was right in the heart of Soho. Andrew, Joy and the children, were overcrowded in their single bedroomed Marshall Street home. 53 Kemp House was ideal for them.

The decor, kitchen and bathroom were all dated, and in need of attention. A workforce was organized, and the decoration begun. Many hands made light work, and the flat became attractively bright and fresh within weeks. The kitchen and bathroom were thoroughly cleaned but not updated at that time. Carpet was laid throughout. One of the loveliest periods of our church life together were the many Sunday afternoons spent in the home, enjoying a fellowship lunch, and the celebration of the Lord's Supper.

These significant developments did a great deal to heal our recent disappointments and losses. We were growing again.

The congregation in Soho in 1999

A bridge too far?

It was impossible to work in Soho without regularly encountering the leaders of the two Catholic churches and St Anne's, the parish church. An estimated five thousand residents lived in Soho and a high proportion were Catholic: Spanish, Italian, Irish and Polish. Jews, Chinese, and Bangladeshi families were also being accommodated in Soho Housing Association property.

With the rebuilding of the bombed St Anne's, and the arrival of new church leaders in the communities around Soho, ecumenism became an issue. We would not become involved as a church in any planned service activities, but I felt inclined to accept the invitation to meet with the ministers and clergy as an individual. Two activities drew us together.

An ecumenical breakfast!

The first was a monthly breakfast, usually held in one or the other of the priests' fine, Georgian homes. Meeting at 8 am on the first Monday of the month, we sat on beautiful Chippendale carved chairs and ate from lovely mahogany tables. We were served by nuns and housekeepers. The group included the ministers and clergy of the Catholic, Methodist, General Baptist, Anglican, Church of Scotland, and the American church in London. Breakfast was spent talking generally with those sitting on either side. This done, there was an open time of sharing of what was happening in our churches, leading to a Bible reading, comment, and prayer by our host or nominated guest.

Apart from two of the ministers, I was left on the fringe of the gathering. The work I was doing, and the church I was leading, was known to all. We were attracting some of their congregation to our own services, which may have soured the atmosphere. Very little of the general conversation was shared, as the guest on either side tended to talk to the other person sitting next to them! The Scripture I chose to read, my comment, and how I chose to pray, also isolated me. The evangelical view was not welcome. More than once, one of the leaders criticized me publicly for what I had shared when he followed on at the next breakfast—but every Christmas Day he came to our home to give us his greeting personally. And the minister of Bloomsbury Baptist Church announced in the presence of the entire group that he and I had very little in common, but he respected me for doing what I felt to be God's will!

At least I had the respect of two of the men: the Methodist Superintendent from Hind Street, Marylebone and the pastor leading the American Church in the Whitefield Memorial Church, Tottenham Court Road. The latter never once spoke out in my support, but privately indicated his shared faith. He invited me to lunch at his Grosvenor Square Club in the weeks before my retirement! I must have made an impression on one of the nuns who came to our home just before we left and kissed me as we parted.

Looking back, I wish I had done more, not less, to be a witness to the members of this group. Several of them were lone, single men. They had their beautiful homes and furniture but not the joys of family life. More time spent with them as individuals, inviting them to our home, and showing Christian love and hospitality may have been more productive than engaging in spiky debates.

An ecumenical Easter!

The second ecumenical activity was more challenging. It arose from the breakfast sessions and was a proposal to hold a series of public meetings to 'Prepare for Passiontide and Easter in Soho.' These would be held at the St Patrick's Church in Soho Square in the early evening on the five Mondays preceding Easter weekend. Five representatives of the breakfast group would speak to an aspect of the general theme: 'Why did he die on the cross?' Each session would conclude with discussion and prayer.

Was it wise to get involved as an individual minister in a public activity with others of mixed understanding of Jesus' death? I was invited to take the lead session and agreed. I had the choice of theme, within the overall title. I went for: Jesus dying as 'A Substitute' for guilty sinners. Others elected to speak on Jesus, 'A Second Adam', 'A Healer', 'A Liberator', and 'An Exemplar'.

Some of the talks were more directly Biblical than others, but I was thankful for the opportunity to contribute to the series, and to such a mixed audience. Some of the other sessions were less helpful, and which only served to demonstrate the wide differences of theology in the group.

To complete the challenge, and to ratchet up the issues of associating with non-evangelicals, there was also the regular invitation to take a Bible reading at the annual Carol Service at the Church of Our Lady of the Assumption, Golden Square. The church featured in Dickens' *Barnaby Rudge* and is devoted to the virgin Mary. Inside, a crowned statue presents the mother of Jesus as the Queen of Heaven! The Carol Service pulled out all the stops: a hired classical choir, seven readings all read by local ministers and clergy, and a selection of the choicest of traditional carols. The priest hosted a generous reception afterwards. I received an invitation to read a lesson on several occasions and, after considerable heart-searching, agreed on each occasion but one. There was much to ignore and a certain risk, but I read the account of the incarnation as clearly and meaningfully as possible in a building packed with my Catholic neighbours. It was a difficult decision to take part, but for me the privilege of handling the Bible's message was too great to refuse.

I know that not all would agree with my policy in relating to others of a very different theological standing. Perhaps I was wrong, but my decision was with the highest intention.

The Word alive

Our ministry for the church in Soho was Bible-based and normally handled in an expository way whole passages, books, Gospels, and Letters at a time—in increasing depth as believers, and the congregation, grew in knowledge and understanding.

At its formation, the church had accepted the reformed and orthodox view of Scripture summarized in 2 Timothy 3:16: 'All Scripture is God-breathed and is useful for teaching, rebuking, correcting and training in righteousness, so that the man/woman of God may be thoroughly equipped for every good work.' Having embraced this truth, Scripture was always going to have a primary place in every service and meeting. Given our circumstances, nothing gave me greater joy than to go to every possible length, and by using every means available, to explain and apply the Bible's message to those who had come to hear it—many for the first time.

> Scripture was always going to have a primary place in every service and meeting

The thematic programmes below give a glimpse of some of what was attempted over an eighteen-year period on Sunday morning, evening, and midweek meetings. Those with an asterisk were midweek.

Truth on Trial: 25 Sunday morning talks on the Letter to the Romans.
Paul writes to the Christians in Thessalonica: 13 studies on the first and second letters.*
The Genius of Genesis: 36 Sunday morning illustrated talks on chapters 1 to 4.
The Home that God Built: 5 talks on our home, marriage and family from a biblical perspective.

Key words of the Bible: 6 illustrated talks on Sin, Redemption, Justification, Regeneration, Repentance, and Faith.

A complete Bible overview: 66 studies on the Old and New Testament books over three years.

The Evidence for believing that Jesus is the Christ: 5 talks from Matthew's Gospel: He was born into the right family. He was conceived by the Holy Spirit. He was born in the right place. He was called out of the right country. He grew up in the right village.

When God Hides his Face: 5 talks on the life and ministry of Elijah in a secular age.*

Encouragement for Exiles: 32 studies in 1 and 2 Peter.*

Jude's Jewel: 11 studies in the Letter which urges believers to 'contend earnestly for the faith.'*

Complete in Christ: 6 studies in the Letter to the Colossians.*

Haggai—the man with a message for today's church: 5 studies in 'What God expects in a day of small things.'*

Getting the most from your Bible: 8 studies in interpreting and applying the Bible's message.*

Living with Love—1 Corinthians 13: 10 devotional talks given at the Communion Service.

Paul's Letter to Titus: 5 studies under the title 'Guiding the Pastor'.*

The Calvary Road: 14 studies in Mark's Gospel, tracing the journey of Jesus from his Baptism to his Ascension.

Christianity Rediscovered: 7 studies uncovering the truth about the Christian faith in Acts.

The Gospel by John: 42 studies given occasionally over 3 years.

Essential Christianity: 12 studies covering the whole gospel by Mark, with an introduction to each study, notes to guide group leaders, an outline of the passage to guide group discussion, and a conclusion, underlining the truths to be grasped about Jesus.

This last series came into being as the result of an unexpected influx of Soho mothers one Sunday morning, anxious to get their children into a Church School the following September! Rather than continue our usual series, it seemed more helpful to provide something basic for them based on Mark's Gospel. The younger members of the congregation, with the mothers, were divided into smaller, less formal groups, with a leader to steer them through the morning's passage. We had just a week to organize and prepare this series, notes as well.

The congregation of Immanuel in 1993 following one of the last of the Broadwick Street Sunday Services. For a few weeks we had access to the Marshall Street Health Clinic, having failed to secure the use of the Charles Norton Centre.

A pattern emerged along these lines: a seven-minute introduction to the morning's theme, twenty minutes for the groups to discuss the passage, all come back together to share a ten-minute application of the lessons we should be learning. All the notes used were bound into a personalized record of the teaching received. These were eventually given to those who had taken part. No doubt everything could have been done much better if we had had a little more time. I was encouraged that the membership was flexible enough, without notice, to turn the entire service round to accommodate the sudden influx of visitors.

Chapter 13

Printed and bound sets of notes were a feature of most of what we did, especially during the last few years of my time in Soho. I committed myself to attempting to encourage the church to grow together as the body of Christ. For a variety of reasons there was a great deal of coming and going, but hopefully the shared notes enabled us to stay in touch as we journeyed on together.

Challenges

We were busy in the church family, but still involved in local lives. Our member, Carol, had met and married her husband during the time he was based in the Philippines as an American soldier. At some point in the past they arrived in Soho, making their home in Ingestre Court. It was an uneasy relationship but in later life they found they needed each other. Carol, having become a believer, would occasionally invite me to the home, warning that Jim was a hardened atheist. I made sure I was on my best behaviour, slowly attempting to build a relationship with him, while not wrecking the opportunity by engaging him in gospel issues too quickly. This was a long-term task.

Jim was elderly, frail, and yet tough as old boots! He had served as a professional soldier in an Administrative Unit of the United States Army over many years. I soon discovered that his passion was the care of his financial assets. Every day involved a microscopic examination of the investment pages: his stocks going up, and down. The money was firmly guarded against all attempts by Carol to provide for her family at home and visiting them at least occasionally. Jim acknowledged the money would be hers eventually, but not while he was alive.

There was regular friction in the home. Eventually it reached the stage where Carol was told to pack and leave for the Philippines. This may have been the time the church was asked to fund the flight, which we did for her sake. I maintained a general contact with Jim following this upset, although he didn't have a good word to say about the church. Things were to deteriorate considerably sometime later. Jim wasn't a fit man, and was dependent on a District Nurse, Home Help and meals delivered to the home.

One Saturday afternoon, months after Carol's departure, I received a furious telephone call from Jim. He wanted to see me: 'Get round here, now!' he demanded. I had no idea what the problem could be but was there in a few minutes. Jim met me at the front door of the flat, his face a picture of foul rage. As soon as the door was closed a torrent of personal abuse flooded out of him, and just kept on coming. He reached back into his old army days for the language with which to accuse, shame and humble me. It was a long time before the filthy flood stopped long enough for me to ask what I had done. At last he leant back in his chair, totally exhausted. Gradually, the truth came out. He had been searching through Carol's personal correspondence in her absence and had discovered a letter that I had written to her while she was in the Philippines. She had written to me to ask if she should return and care for Jim in his frail state? Was he seriously ill? Unbeknown to me, Jim had also written to Carol and had asked her to return, saying he was very ill. Naturally, she didn't want to return only to face another rejection soon after. So, how ill was Jim? I had told her he was managing fairly well, with support. I had seen him recently managing to get to the chute with his rubbish. I could say no more.

Jim raged, digging deeper still into the cesspit to find more vile language to throw at me. How dare I pass judgement on his ability to manage, and comment on the state of his health and needs, he wanted to know. Perhaps he had a point. I was feeling as if the contents of a filthy bucket had been thrown over me. I attempted to apologize sincerely several times, without making the slightest impact on the situation. At last the tirade dried up, and I was shown to the door and made my way home, feeling totally crushed. Was I spiritually qualified to take the lead in the services the following day? Should I hand over to Andrew? The whole experience hung over me for a long time, seriously affecting my energy for the wider work we were doing.

Carol returned not long after, embarrassed that she had left the personal correspondence where it could be found, read and used against the church and me. It was sometime later that Jim had a stroke, and lay dying in St Mary's Hospital, Paddington. He was in no shape to ask me to visit, it was probably Carol who suggested I went. There was an opportunity to talk quietly with Jim, trying to repair the damage done that Saturday afternoon, months earlier. I read to him, pointing him to the God of all compassion and the Saviour of sinners who loved him and gave himself for him. Jim remained silent, non-responsive—until I began to pray. Then there was a distinct squeeze from the hand I was holding. That's all. Jim died later that night. Now, the money was Carol's, and she returned to the Philippines once Jim's affairs were wound up.

Caring for outside members

The Soho church became known among believers which led to our having contact with a circle of Christians who were part of other London congregations. They could be time-consuming as they became regular visitors to our home. Steve was one of these. A graduate of Durham University, he was being fast-tracked toward the rank of a Police Inspector. He was married with a young daughter and a member of a large congregation in the City. He was concerned about issues relating to his family and working life, and needed help in applying the Bible's teaching to those areas. Steve felt a strong attraction for the preaching he enjoyed in his large, student congregation, but lacked a pastor who would give him the time to deal with his questions.

Juliette was another believer, rather like Steve. Before coming to live in St James' Residences, she had joined a church in Notting Hill, and continued to worship there. Juliette was a small, strong Mexican woman, who had met and married her English husband while he was teaching in her home town. Later, they moved to London, and became neighbours of ours. It wasn't a happy home, largely because her husband was a schizophrenic and an unbeliever. Juliette herself claimed to have visions and that evil spirits were active within the home. There was frequent tension, usually followed by a buzz at our door. One night, Juliette became ill and took to her bed.

At some point she woke to find her husband leaning over her with a paper knife in his hand. She grabbed some essentials and rushed across the courtyard to our home. The frantic buzzing of the doorbell woke us with a start. Juliette came in, sharing her story and asking to spend the night safely in our home. With Jon married, his room was available, so Pam prepared the bed for our visitor. The rest of the night was uneventful. Juliette was still too afraid to return home the following morning, so she stayed while I went to see her husband.

He had always been polite and we had talked often when meeting at the gate. Now our relationship was strained and difficult. It was clear that the marriage was at an end. He assured me he meant no harm to Juliette and understood that she would probably return to Mexico now. I visited the husband occasionally, and eventually trust was restored. He continued writing to me way past retirement.

As suspected, Juliette decided to return to Mexico, letting us know that she had arrived and had settled into a suitable church. What was extraordinary was that six months later there was a call on the intercom one Sunday afternoon. I went down to the gate to check who was there. A young Mexican, dressed in black, stood waiting, with a crumpled piece of paper in his hand with my name and address on it. Apparently, Juliette had told him before leaving Mexico that if he was ever in trouble in London he was to go and see Michael. The young man stayed for two or three days, but then landed himself a job: advertising a Mexican Restaurant in the street, dressed for the part, in a large sombrero. We didn't get to meet him again.

A card on the kiosk

I had noticed a local newspaper kiosk, which had a glass-fronted notice board, displaying post-card sized advertisements of the Soho kind. The thought occurred to me that if these women were able to advertise what they had to offer, then why shouldn't we share Good News here. The cost was minimal and, having chosen a suitable text, the card went on display. Its message was straightforward:

> 'This is love: not that we loved God,
> but that he loved us, and sent his Son to be
> the means whereby our sins can be forgiven,'
> I JOHN 4:10
> Rev Michael Toogood
> IMMANUEL COMMUNITY CHURCH in SOHO
> We meet on Sundays at 10.30am in the
> CHARLES NORTON CENTRE
> Broadwick Street, W1

Brian lived in West London but he had Soho in his blood. For many years he had done remarkable work in his small studio on the corner of Brewer

Street and Wardour Street. He was a highly skilled film editor, working long hours to meet hard deadlines. Working to a tight script, he would edit many hours of film down to whatever time was available—perhaps an hour-long television programme. Sadly, Brian was an alcoholic. Although, somehow, maintaining his work, his drinking had cost him his marriage and two daughters. One night, he wrapped his BMW round a tree, and blamed the police for chasing him. Life had reached a new low.

Brian travelled back into the West End on a Sunday morning from his West London home, and stepped into the Norton Centre. He sat in the front row, listening. He came to join us for the next eleven weeks without a break. Over coffee he asked if we might meet up during the week and talk over a few things he had in mind. Tuesday at 10 am was fine. Come the day, the coffee was ready, and two Bibles close at hand. It was a relaxed atmosphere. Brian made himself at home in a comfortable chair. He felt the need to put everything about himself 'on the table'.

He had served in the RAF during his National Service and had been billeted with Christians, whom he despised. He went out of his way to make life a misery for them and was never happier than when he caught them out or embarrassed them in some way. Back in civvy street again, he pressed on with his career and made progress. With a wife, a home in London, and two daughters, life should have been great, but alcohol gradually began to dominate the working day and nights. Eventually, Brian was compelled to face the cost of his addiction in terms of those he loved, and the home which sheltered him. Having lost everything, he was reduced to sleeping on the floor of his studio, and somehow getting through the day. The situation was complicated by his involvement in the local clubs and brothels. These were an irresistible pull.

We poured a second cup of coffee, and Brian continued with his story. One night, deeply depressed (alcohol is a depressant) and being utterly helpless, Brian felt life was not worth living. Anything was better than this. He made his way from his studio, along Brewer Street, turning right up Great Poulteney Street, intending to make his way to Oxford Circus Underground Station where it would take just one step off the platform to end it all. It then dawned on him he was too early because the system was not running for some time yet. Brian paused, and noticed the glass fronted notice-board, with the post-cards displayed. He recognized a few of the names, and had probably used them at some time in the past, but now one stood out: 'This is love; not that we loved God but that he loved us and sent his Son to be the means whereby our sins can be forgiven...' Brian stepped back, and felt that this message was for him. Could there be help, forgiveness, and a new start? He checked out our details and determined to track us down the following Sunday.

Preachers can tell when members of the congregation are listening, and Brian certainly was during his Sunday morning visits. He had picked up a Bible expression which I think was mentioned on a summer Sunday morning while I was battling with pneumonia. My right-hand man was away, and I just had to get through somehow before getting home to bed. The phrase which impressed Brian was 'Abraham believed God, and it was credited to him as righteousness' (Romans 4:3).

He was keenly aware of his wretched, degraded state and the depths to which he had fallen. I explained that none of us were righteous, even if we were striving to achieve it. The problem wasn't only what we did which fails us, but what we are as fallen human beings. Romans 4:3 could help us. The apostle looks back to Genesis 15:6, when God promised childless Abraham that he would have descendants, as many as the stars in the sky. It was the fact that Abraham believed God's promise that brought him into a righteous relationship with him. I pointed out that God continues to promise that he will regard us as righteous and give us his peace because of what Jesus has done for us in his death on the cross. Brian's joy was profound. He believed and trusted in Christ for himself. It was a lovely moment.

But he would need support and regular contact for some time to come. He also felt that he needed the support that Alcoholics Anonymous could give him, and regularly attended a lunch-time session at the nearby Middlesex Hospital. I'm not sure how he made it possible, but I was invited to be part of the group on one occasion. The only condition was that I did not speak. The experience was deeply instructive. The first thing that registered was that the group members were not 'old lags' but smart young businessmen and attractive female professionals. Each contributed in turn, all beginning by stating their name, and admitting that they were alcoholics.

Challenges

Brian remained in close contact with us for a considerable time, until he discovered that he had a Baptist church almost on his doorstep. It was known to us and was regarded as a solid and sound Bible teaching fellowship. Brian was received as a member, and, after some years, became its Treasurer. Much later, I was sorry to hear that Brian had resigned as Treasurer and stepped back from membership. It wasn't that he had backslidden, returning to alcohol and the clubs, he simply felt that his spiritual life had been crushed by the narrowness and joylessness of his church. I had some sympathy with that, having taken deputation meetings there on a number of occasions. The church seemed so 'Independent and Reformed' that they could only bring themselves to associate with two other churches in the country! I'm trusting that this is not the end of the story for Brian.

A challenge to my past

God's Word continued to work among us. By the mid-1990s our congregation was building again and no longer did we feel lost in the School Hall. Mr and Mrs Browning, the Superintendent of the Peabody Buildings in Mayfair, began to attend. One or two mothers who were familiar with the venue through their contact with the School joined us. A Taiwanese mother attended with her young daughter. She proved to be the link between her new neighbours and the church when, one summer's morning, she arrived and introduced them to us: father, mother, and the most beautiful little doll-like daughter. They were Japanese.

I liked to be at the door to greet the congregation, always on the look-out for someone new, or hovering around the entrance. I shook the couple's hand, told them they were very welcome, and said hello to the little girl. The couple were immaculately dressed and, of course, had perfect manners. Suddenly, I was aware of a strange disturbance somewhere inside me but couldn't account for it immediately. It was only later that it dawned on me where this 'disturbance' originated.

I was four years old when my family suddenly faced upheaval. It was 1941 and dark war clouds cast a deep shadow over us all. My father was nearing the point when he would be regarded as being too old for active Service, but his 'call-up' papers arrived. He was sent to Aldershot for basic training before being enlisted in the Royal Artillery. He spent three months training on Salisbury Plain before coming home for embarkation leave. I vividly remember the day my mother, three sisters and I went with him to the railway station to say goodbye. Dad kissed us, climbed aboard, and waved until the train was out of sight. We had no idea where he was going or that we wouldn't meet again for four years.

Travelling from London to Portsmouth, my father joined thousands of other soldiers on a troop ship sailing to Singapore. However, Singapore fell to the Japanese in February 1942 before the troop ship arrived and it was redirected to India, where another crisis had already arisen. In December 1941, the Japanese had first bombed and then invaded Rangoon in the south of Burma. The British-led Burma Army consisted of only two Divisions, and these were poorly armed and equipped. They were no match for the battle-hardened invaders who eventually drove them 900 miles north into India. The long road was littered with some 80,000 bodies of soldiers and the thousands of Indians who had been employed in the South. This was the greatest retreat in British history.

My father arrived in India shortly after this debacle. Burma was firmly in the hands of the Japanese now, and it would take two years of arduous training in the monsoon as well as the dry season before a new strike force, the 14th Army, could consider confronting the enemy once more. Japan would surrender on 15 August 1945, but only after suffering defeat in three major battles in the Arakan, Imphal and Kohima. There were more Victoria Crosses awarded in the Burma conflict than any other arena of the second World War.

My father, who was serving with a Royal Artillery unit, part of the 7th Indian Division, was involved in the first of the three battles. The Division was spearheading the advance into the Arakan when it was surrounded by a large force of Japanese. Records of the event are varied and grim, but for twenty-one days the Division was subjected to attack day and night, including hand-to-hand fighting. The official account records:

'The flimsy defences held, because no soldier would yield; they fought or died where they stood. How some of them died will for ever be a blot on the stained honour of the Japanese Army. On the 7th February, 1944, yelling Japanese overran the main dressing station, crowded with the wounded, and with the surgeons still operating. The helpless men on their stretchers were slaughtered in cold blood, the doctors were lined up and shot, the orderlies made to carry the Japanese wounded back, then also murdered. A counterattack by British forces the next morning exacted retribution, but found the hospital a shambles, the only survivors being a few wounded men who had rolled into the jungle and shammed death.'

My father was one of only three survivors! He was rescued by a fearless Gurkha soldier who fought his way into the field hospital, lifted him bodily from his bed, and carried him to the safety of the jungle. The 7th Indian Division held out while the Japanese began to suffer starvation, having failed to capture essential food and ammunition. Eventually, they began to withdraw, leaving behind 6,000 dead. It was Friday, 25 February 1944 when the siege was broken. The British forces had lost 3,506 men, more than half of that number coming from the 7th Indian Division.

In his book, *Burma '44*, James Holland claims that the victory in the Arakan was the battle that 'turned Britain's War in the East'. Like Montgomery's victory at El Alamein, it turned the tide, stopped an oncoming flood and led to final victory.

My father came home in the autumn of 1945. He was never well, and there was no after-care. He had been starved, diseased, hospitalized, and had survived the horrors of jungle warfare for four years. He returned home to rejuvenate the family dairy and lived until he was 81. Widowed in 1962, he died in 1987, and is buried with my mother in the City Cemetery, Cambridge.

All this lay in the background of my mind as I welcomed the Japanese family to our morning service. It was the wife and mother who began to meet for prayer and study on Tuesday evenings as well as Sunday mornings. Kanako was bright and attentive and had no great problem with the English language. We were, of course, already attempting to speak clearly, trying to communicate the message to those for whom the Bible was unknown.

After just a few weeks, Kanako said she understood what Andrew and I had been teaching on Sundays and mid-week and had received Jesus Christ as her Saviour. She had grasped that to be a disciple of Jesus meant becoming a learner, a follower and his servant. She had already worked out that to believe in Jesus also required her to be baptized into him like those she had seen being baptized in a river in Japan. Would we baptize her? Yes, we would, but probably not in the Thames. We approached our nearest friends and neighbours in Shaftesbury Avenue regarding the use of their pool. Both congregations held their own morning services, then came together to witness Kanako's baptism.

Working through this later I recognized this as a deep-rooted resentment against the Japanese because of their unbelievable cruelty during the War, the suffering caused to my father (and millions of others) and the anxiety and stress caused to my mother over the four-year period my father was away. We all bore deep emotional scars as family members because of what our father had been through. It wasn't too much to ask that the family be allowed to sit in the congregation, and share our worship and teaching, but now there was a request to enter into believer's baptism, church membership, share the Lord's Supper, becoming one of us.

The church recognized the grace of God in Kanako, and I couldn't stand in the way. The arrangements were made, and the baptism took place. It wasn't until I lifted Kanako up out of the water, and held her for a moment while she caught her breath, that the Spirit challenged me about my ungracious attitude: 'On what basis did the Lord receive you?' 'Were you more deserving of mercy than Kanako?' 'Was Kanako more responsible than you for atrocities committed in the War?' The deeply humbling questions demanded a response. No, God received me in Christ, by grace alone. No, I was not innocent but a guilty sinner in God's sight, not just because of what I had done, but because of what I was. No, Kanako was not responsible, nor guilty, of the crimes committed by her nation during WW2—she wasn't even born! I felt the antagonism fade, to be replaced by a wonderful sense of us being united in Christ, and to Christ— sinners saved by grace alone!

The family continued meeting with us for some months, before eventually returning to Japan. Letters from Kanako continued for some time. She was happily settled into a good church and was active in its Sunday school. Sadly, the marriage had failed, the husband leaving his wife and young daughter soon after the return.

More encouragements followed that year, 1999, when Joanne Broadhurst and Dr Tim Wakeford sought formal membership with us, having worshipped with us for some time.

An unwelcome invasion

Facing the challenge of the ecumenical situation was one thing but dealing with tension caused by the activities of another Bible believing group was quite a different experience. Home visiting had been fundamental to our work from its inception. We had no ready-made congregation, and no nucleus of a believing membership. Both had to be built by constant visiting, relationship building and practical service. It was a slow task, demanding self-discipline, and not a little courage, given the variety of residents, and the demands of those visited.

> Home visiting had been fundamental to our work from its inception. We had no ready-made congregation, and no nucleus of a believing membership. Both had to be built by constant visiting, relationship building and practical service

A charismatic group began taking an interest in the Soho community during the early 1990s. They had established a large congregation in the Sydenham area of south-east London, based in a large Comprehensive School. By 1982 they had two congregations numbering four hundred people. By the 1990s, new churches, and links forged with existing churches, were spreading across London. Soho was designated as one of the areas where a Sunday congregation would be launched. Their style was to import a sizable group of mainly young people to form an instant congregation to which, hopefully, locals could eventually be added. A cinema in Great Windmill Street was one of the venues used.

None of this affected us, or the work we were doing, until groups of young people began visiting blocks of flats like Blake House. By this time we were known and trusted by many of the residents. It was usual for us to be invited in, sat down, and served cups of coffee. We were trusted with personal issues, money, keys, medication and so on. I once accompanied an elderly Indian woman to her Bank in Holborn, where she wanted to put her family jewels into a vault for safety while she was abroad visiting family. She said the jewels were worth £250,000!

We therefore enjoyed good relationships and had the trust of our neighbours. But then, young people from outside began visiting and succeeded in getting into the building, probably because they were mistaken for our own members. Connie and Ted were among the most seriously affected by this. Mary O'Neil particularly had given so much personal care to Connie, who was confined to a wheelchair with multiple sclerosis. One Saturday afternoon, two very pleasant young women arrived at her door and were invited in. No doubt they were attentive in every way and offered to return the following weekend. What they really wanted was the use of the home where other members could meet and a cell be formed, from which they could reach out to the other homes in the block. They got as far as holding meetings in Connie's home, which went on endlessly, causing Connie great distress. Eventually they were told not to return—and we were no longer made welcome or needed either. Some ten years of trust had disappeared by one invasion.

> Some ten years of trust had disappeared by one invasion

Andrew and I invited the two local leaders to meet with us in our home. It wasn't an easy session. They were young, bright, with that spiritual superiority often found among their kind. One was the grandson of a well-known missionary of the 1950s, his female colleague a lawyer. We pressed our case with, on my part at least, considerable irritation. Afterwards, we weren't aware of them continuing to pursue their policy; rather there seemed to be a withdrawing from the area, leaving a young man in charge of a small bookshop in Green's Court. The group had one great asset: a female team member with a background in the sex industry. She lived among local prostitutes in a flat in Great Windmill Street. Clearly converted, and with a concern for the women still involved, she had a natural access to many of the women which we were not able match.

We managed to repair the damage done to our relationship with Connie and Ted, but to have allowed the situation to continue may well have destroyed a major aspect of our long-term work.

Living with the locals

From the beginning, church members were encouraged to get involved as Christians in the community. Whatever else may have been lacking in Immanuel Community Church we can be encouraged to the degree in which we sought to serve our neighbours through a variety of activities where we lived. In Soho and Mayfair, members played a leading part in their Residents' Associations, two local schools, the Soho Society and Housing Association. Many individuals were supported whenever they found themselves in need.

> From the beginning, church members were encouraged to get involved as Christians in the community

Dr Peltz

Dr Sam Peltz was a local boy who made good. For many years his mother owned a shop in Berwick Street Market, specializing in material of all kinds. On market days, she displayed her wares on a table outside the shop for several hours a day—even when in her 80s. Sam did well and for many years was the lone GP looking after the health of the Soho community. His surgery was in Broadwick Street, near to the spot where the old water pump stood, and where Dr John Snow (1813–1858) discovered that cholera was a waterborne disease. Having become residents, we promptly signed ourselves up as patients with Dr Peltz, and we never regretted it. He may have had little in terms of 'bedside manner' but he inspired confidence by his self-assured manner.

It was Dr Peltz I had to persuade to take Len back onto his books when I undertook to visit and support him every day if he would let Margaret go. Dr Peltz seemed to respect what I was attempting, and, as a Jew, was not put off by my being a Christian.

A replica of the pump where in 1854 Dr John Snow discovered that cholera was a waterborne disease (plaque inset)

An incident significantly strengthened the link between us. We were living in St James' Residences by this time. In the block of flats opposite was a Jewish couple, brother and sister. They were elderly, grossly over-weight, and lived in squalor. They needed their GP to pay them home visits because they were unable to get to the surgery. I got to know the couple well and visited them at home occasionally. Being there one day when the brother was unwell, Dr Peltz was called. He arrived late in the day. There was the problem of getting the prescription made up after hours, but it was no big deal; pharmacists had a rota for out of hours emergencies like this, so I did what was necessary. The GP appreciated this. Needing to see Dr Peltz myself within a few weeks of our meeting, I stepped into the crowded waiting room, just as the GP came into the room to give some paperwork to the receptionist. He looked up, raised an eyebrow, and said to the receptionist: 'When this man comes into the surgery, treat him like the Rabbi, show him straight into my room, he hasn't the time to sit and wait!' I was told to follow him and received the prescription I needed immediately. Needless to say, this hardly endeared me to the other patients who had to wait even longer!

Mary O'Neil made a good impression on the GP's wife, Lois Peltz, our Independent Councillor. A local woman was confined to her home, above shops, in Beak Street, and was finding that local services left a great deal to be desired. She appealed to her local Councillor, who was at a loss to know where help could be found. Having received Mrs Peltz' call, I urged Mary to visit on a regular basis, and Mrs Peltz never forgot the help she gave, speaking of it several years later when meeting her at a reception.

The Bangladeshi family

I have already mentioned the Bangladeshi family who came to live in the flat above us. With the husband serving a long prison sentence, there were issues we were able to resolve over the years. Pam particularly had a good relationship with the wife. Now in their teens, both the young people were a problem: the boy was into drug taking, and inviting white school girlfriends to the home on Saturday mornings when his mother was out. With paper-thin walls it was obvious what was going on in the flat upstairs. The daughter, in her mid-teens, strong and vivacious, got into bad company, and began coming home in the early hours of the morning. When the police began a clean-up of the Soho sex industry and the trade moved to the Kings Cross area, the daughter was involved at some level in this. Deeply concerned about her daughter, the mother sought Pam's support. There were periods when, several nights a week, the girl would arrive home in the early hours of the morning. A noisy row would break out, followed by urgent knocking at our door. Pam was needed upstairs to take on the role of questioning the girl about her experience that evening. Had she had unprotected sex? Could she be infected or pregnant? Did she need to be taken to A&E? Pam found a number of her roles as a minister's wife challenging, yet she shone in tasks like this. Pam did whatever had to be done night after night without complaint.

Just before retiring, we were invited to the home for a beautiful and carefully prepared meal. As their culture dictated, we eating at the table while our hostess, not eating with us, waited on our every need.

Mr Ali the Muslim

We had a good relationship with another Muslim family in the Residences, built up through the work of the Tenants Association. The parents had two growing sons, one of whom had reached the age when a bride was to be sought for him. The whole family intended to fly to Bangladesh, complete the ceremonies, then return with the bride. Mr Ali arrived on the doorstep with the Bridegroom-to-be, and was invited in. He explained the situation: they would be away for about three months. He asked if I would call at the home once or twice a week, check the mail, and pay any outstanding bills. He then handed over a large handful of paper money, and an impressive number of keys, giving access to the entire home. Although not completely sure what the request would involve, I said I would be pleased to do all that was necessary, to ensure the family could return debt free to their secure home.

There were no serious problems, just an amazing amount of mail, sent to a variety of people using this address! All the doors in the home were secured with padlocks. The family eventually returned with a beautiful young bride in tow and kind gifts in lieu of the help given. Perhaps it was significant that with other Muslims living in the area, and a mosque 150 yards away, Mr Ali should entrust his money, keys, and his home, to his Christian neighbour.

'The Last Temptation of Christ'

However, another incident humbled me. In 1988, Martin Scorsese's film *The Last Temptation of Christ* was released and hit the London screens. The Christian press was armed and ready to denounce its blasphemous claim that Mary Magdalene was Jesus' wife. I thought I saw an opportunity for a lead theme for our regular circular, *inTouch*. I wrote the article and we circulated it throughout Soho and Mayfair. Within a few days I received a scorching response from someone living just a couple of streets away. The letter said it was quite clear that I had not seen the film myself and that the film was based on a strong tradition that had been in circulation for many years.

At least the first part of the complaint was true. The second part didn't wash, because traditions are not to be regarded as true just because they have been in circulation for centuries. I needed to reply to my critic who, it seems, was the film critic for the *Telegraph* newspaper. I went to see the film for myself and saw no reason to retract anything I had written, although I was very impressed with the deeply dramatic raising of Lazarus! The next morning I wrote to my correspondent, acknowledging that I should have first seen the film before commenting on it, but insisting that our knowledge of Jesus is most reliably based on the four Gospels. I received no reply but made sure the film critic received a copy of every subsequent edition of *inTouch*.

I am reminded of the morning I listened to 'Desert Island Discs'. The castaway that week was Soho local, Jeffrey Bernard, who wrote a weekly column in *The Spectator*, called, 'Low Life.' I was appalled at his cavalier attitude to his serious health problems including diabetes and continuing to drink heavily in spite of having been hospitalized for detox. His approaching death was mocked and the object of crude jokes. In the urgency of the Bible's warning, 'Man is destined to die once, and after that to face judgement…' (Hebrews 9:27), I visited his home, but with no response.

He was probably in the *Coach and Horses*, sitting in his usual seat at the bar. I felt it would be more effective to write to him, sharing my concern for him following his broadcast and recommending that he read the enclosed booklet, John Blanchard's, *Ultimate Questions*. These were delivered to his home personally in Ingestre Court, but there was no response to this either. Jeffrey Bernard died in 1997.

Jack and Pascal's hair saloon

There were also challenges of a different kind. As part of our policy of living with and like our Soho neighbours, we shopped locally whenever possible. For me, it meant getting a haircut at Jack and Pascal's saloon, on the first floor of a multipurpose building in Berwick Street. Looking back, it was as much a challenge going in and coming out as sitting in the hairdresser's chair! The building had a dodgy atmosphere about it, largely because of the other dubious activities that went on there.

Jack and Pascal were as different as chalk and cheese. Jack was a Greek Cypriot, the elder of the two, a family man, who lived up the Edgware Road. Pascal was a Sicilian, who had fingers in many pies. It wasn't unusual to climb the stairs, enter the salon and find it empty because Pascal was out in the street, playing poker with his market friends. Jack was the steadying influence, a nice family man. Pascal lived by the seat of his pants. Almost anything could be bought in this establishment on the quiet, including Rolex watches. There was a lot of whispering in corners, and some burly, well-dressed customers, who didn't appear to pay.

I was in the chair one day, with Pascal in charge of the hair cutting. Clearly his mind wasn't on the job and he was distracted by an attractive young mum who had brought her small son for his first haircut. Pascal was going through the motions, more interested in who was behind him. He reached up to a shelf and took down a container of mousse. Still watching the woman in the mirror, he pressed the nozzle, spraying its contents into his hand. A mound of brilliant orange foam appeared, increasing in size. It was about to be massaged into my hair, before he suddenly realised he'd made a serious mistake. I didn't understand his Sicilian remark. My parting may have been on the wrong side, but I thought it best to cut my losses, pay, and escape the premises.

Lee the glue sniffer

Lee presented a challenge of another kind. At one point we found short films made by a company called Lamp Productions were helpful to the epilogue part of the youth programme on Friday evenings. Hearing of our work in Soho, the CEO of Lamp Productions came to visit. He was an evangelical Christian and we spent an hour over coffee exchanging ways in which we were seeking to share the good news of Jesus Christ. One morning, when travelling into the West End by underground, he was confronted by Lee who was begging. The film maker stopped, told Lee that there was little he could do to help, but that he knew a man who could. They walked together from Piccadilly to our gate in Brewer Street. Having pressed the bell, and introduced the young man, the CEO guided him into the courtyard, then hurried on to his appointment. Lee came in and we settled in the study.

Lee was reeking not only of the filth of the streets, but it was obvious that he was a glue sniffer. Like his fellow addicts, Lee's most treasured possessions were two or three plastic shopping bags, one inside of the other, containing the contents of a number of tubes of glue. The size of the bags made it possible to cover the mouth and nose, while inhaling deeply. The fumes given off by the glue aggravate the addict's eyes, nose, throat, and eventually the brain. Lee was a hardened 'sniffer'.

Lee had been on the streets since the age of seventeen. The memory of his father was lost in the mists of time and glue. A new man had come into the home, they didn't get on, so Lee left. He was now twenty-two, homeless and a loner. He felt safer on his own and had learned how to 'get by'. He had a variety of preferred places to spend the night, mostly north of Oxford Street. The last time he came to our home, he said he had woken up early, thinking to himself how wonderful it was to be so free with no responsibilities. Before leaving his night shelter, a woman had passed by and given him a £50 note! He looked around my study, with its grey carpet, mustard coloured walls, white paintwork, books, inherited antique furniture, and said he would love a room like that. Remembering his earlier comment on the joy of being footloose and free, I hinted at the cost of such luxury—around £100 a week.

Over the months, our relationship became open and honest. I could challenge him, advise him, and share the gospel with him, only to find his brain was addled and incapable of reasoning or making any sense of what was said to him. It was the last time we met, before I retired. He asked if he could use the bathroom. He was gone some time and left soon after returning to the study. I saw him through the security doors, shook him by the hand and said goodbye, commending him to the God of all grace. Lee stepped out into the bustling street and was gone. I went indoors and got straight on with whatever I had been doing before Lee arrived, thinking nothing of the bathroom. Pam came home later, and immediately detected the fumes from the glue. She never shared what she found in the bathroom, but she spent a couple of hours disinfecting and cleaning every part of it. Towels and the cushion Lee had been sitting on in the study were taken and put in the washing machine.

'The Country's Most Violent Criminal'

One Friday evening, with the youth groups over, and most of the members collected by parents, there was one boy left. Andrew and Jon having worked all day, it was right for them to get home for a meal, and for me to stay and wait for the boy's mother. He was one of the Play Centre lads who really enjoyed the art and crafts we used to do there. Not being the easiest child to control, his mother appreciated that we had managed to engage him in something worthwhile. At one point, the boy had left the school to become a student at Christ's Hospital, a Public School near Horsham, Sussex. As a boarder, the terms were shorter than regular schools. Having known the lad for several years, and knowing the struggle his mother had with him at home and working too, we were happy for him to join us at the Boys Own Club. 8 pm came and went. 9 pm and still no sign of the mother. Thankfully the school play area was well equipped with climbing frames, so the boy was under no pressure. At 9.20 pm the school gate opened, and the mother came in with a tall, well-built man. She either had no idea she was so late or didn't care. She had been enjoying the evening drinking in a local wine bar. She did say 'thank you' for staying back with her son, and then introduced me to her companion. 'This is John,' she said. The play area was in deep shadow, but I recognized the face immediately. We shook hands, mine small and pathetic, his big, strong, and rough! 'Glad to meet you, John,' I said. They moved off quickly together, the boy tagging along.

John was known in the press as 'The Country's Most Violent Criminal' having spent more than half his age behind bars for violence in various forms. There had been the book and a film. And now he was here, having got close to a vulnerable single mum in a wine bar on a dark winter's night. John may well have been the latest to have been invited in for the night. The last I heard of him was that he had broken the nose of a neighbour in some domestic dispute. This lad was not the only Club member who had to cope with the merry-go-round of come-and-go relationships at home.

Alerts!

Terrorism, terrorist attacks and violence are all part of London life. Around one hundred IRA and other violent attacks took place between 1980 and 2000.

Two incidents were especially local to us in the 1990s. The first was around 8.30 am on 6 April 1992, just when Soho was coming to normal life: workers hurrying to their offices, and parents and children making their way to the Parish School in Great Windmill Street. Bridle Lane is a narrow, one-way street linking Brewer and Beak Streets. Nearby Golden Square (possibly once 'Gelding Square') had a history of horses, stables and carriages. Bridle Lane may well have provided the tack rooms, workshops and grooms' accommodation. More recently, the street was lined with offices and some Soho Housing Association property.

A small IRA bomb was detonated a few yards from the junction of Brewer Street and Bridle Lane, achieving only damage to buildings and immediate windows. It could have been much worse. A company showroom had a large window fronting onto Bridle Lane. An attractive young receptionist usually sat behind her desk just inside. Thankfully the blast sucked the glass into the street, leaving the woman shaken but not injured; the incident would have been deadly if the glass had been blown into the building. There was no obvious reason for placing the bomb there. The most likely explanation seemed to be that it was intended for the Police House in Broadwick Street, but for some reason was not able to be placed there. The police cordoned off the area for several hours which gave me time to write personal letters to the residents living there, offering practical help should it be needed.

The second explosion was on the 30 April 1999. We were enjoying the usual Friday evening Youth Night, with both boys and girls sharing facilities at the parish school. Before long, parents would have been arriving to collect their children, some of them passing the scene. Thankfully, a series of telephone warnings and a police alert let us know there was a problem and warned that we should keep the young people within the school until receiving the all-clear. Although bombs were unusual, at least on two occasions the school play-centre went into lock-down because an armed man was thought to be in the vicinity. So, these alarms were not unknown.

Later we discovered that a nail bomb had been detonated in the Admiral Duncan pub, in Old Compton Street. Three people had been killed and thirty injured. The culprit, David Copeland, had Neo-Nazi convictions and had already planted two other bombs in Brixton and Whitechapel. Copeland was arrested later the same evening and was eventually condemned to six life sentences.

The Admiral Duncan pub after the bombing

Succession planning

It was 1998. We had two years before Pam and I were expecting to retire. This was never going to be a simple case of '65, time up, off you go.' There were good reasons for considering a change of leadership. I had promised Pam, when we embraced the Soho project, that I would do all I could not to spend our retirement years in Central London. After eighteen years, she felt the need for a radical change of circumstances and an opportunity to live more normally. Like others, she had been stepping over urine and avoiding vomit for those eighteen years. For me there were the dual issues of whether the church needed a change of leadership, in the hope of gaining new vision—men can stay too long in a leadership role—and also, my increasing signs of ill health which, more than once, involved Andrew calling on a Sunday morning to pick up my sermon notes to preach from when a chest infection developed overnight. Central London was not the best environment for someone with weak lungs. The conclusion was that a replacement leader was the way ahead for us.

Andrew and I worked out a series of principles to guide us, having agreed that it would involve seeking a man from outside the existing membership. We would consider one suitably gifted and experienced man at a time, reaching a conclusion with him before moving on to another. We would initially invite him to meet with us, in Soho, where we could recount the origins of the work, and the character of the church planted there, explaining its life and commitment to outreach into the community, before exploring the need for a vision for the future development of the church.

We felt these issues were fundamental, and should precede any invitation to meet the church, or for us to hear the man preach. We were ready to

SOHO
is a piece of cake!

That will come as a surprise to those think Soho is only about sex!

In fact, we boast a variety of classy restaurants, sandwich bars, theme cafes, coffee houses, wine bars, 54 pubs, cinemas, theatres, several hotels, two street markets and a school.

Look a little more closely and, here and there, you will see evidence of normal community life among Soho's residents

This small, central London village boasts a history second to none. Local physician, Dr John Snow, discovered that cholera is a water-borne disease. John Logie Baird succeeded in demonstrating television in Frith Street in 1926. Mozart and Handel both had strong links in the area. Furniture designer, Thomas Sheraton had a workshop in Wardour Street. Karl Marx lived in Dean Street and lectured weekly in the Red Lion pub in Great Windmill Street.

It would be nice to think that the many thousands who crowd our streets every day were only here for the culture and cuisine. It must be admitted that Soho continues to promote its reputation as Britain's primary vice area. About 90 clubs offer a variety of erotic entertainment. 65 brothels

advertise their presence in the time honoured way. Prostitution, drug dealing and street begging makes local streets a hazard.

Immanuel is the only indigenous evangelical church in the community. 17 years on from initial evangelistic work, a church has been formed, a full programme of Bible teaching and youth work established, and many avenues of evangelism opened.

Michael Toogood completes his ministry in Soho in January, 2001, so within the next twelve months we are seeking to appoint an additional elder. He will have leadership experience and be willing to build on the existing foundation. He must have the ability to teach the Bible and give pastoral care. With his family's support he must be willing to persevere in a challenging situation. Above all he must have an evangelist's heart, with the energy and vision to lead the church in extending Christian witness within the community.

The work in Soho continues to enjoy wonderful support from many loyal churches and individual believers throughout the country.

Could the Lord be calling you? An elder in your church? Or someone you can recommend to us?

'Where sin increased, grace increased all the more' Romans 5:20

IMMANUEL
THE CHURCH AT THE HEART OF THE SOHO COMMUNITY
- Elders: MICHAEL TOOGOOD ANDREW MURRAY
26 St James Residences 23 Brewer Street London W1R 3FF
0171 434 4056

Two of the appeals in 1999 to find a new leader for the Soho work

 **inContact EXTRA**

begin. It would have been ideal to call a man who was both gifted in preaching and church leadership, as well as being a proven evangelist, but it doesn't often work out like that. Eventually, we approached a man of proven ability in the realm of ministry and church leadership, then waited, covering the whole issue with prayer. All credit to him, he gave time to our invitation to come and explore the Lord's will with us, before concluding that he felt it right to remain where he was, feeding and leading a growing church.

Over the next two years, five other men were carefully and prayerfully considered. Unknown to us, two of the men were already committed to ministry elsewhere, one overseas. One man came to look at Soho, without telling us, and concluded it was not for him. It may have been the same man, or another, who considered responding to our invitation to come and pray, but whose wife said neither she nor the children would be coming with him if he responded to our call. Another declined the invitation to come and talk but regretted it sometime later.

Our *inContact* extra updates at the time were headed in bold fonts, 'We are not looking for another MICHAEL TOOGOOD thank you!' and 'SOHO is a piece of cake!' and another, 'So you want to serve the Lord on the MISSION FIELD? You can!'

There was not a single application or recommendation, except for a couple from a thriving church in a university city who were looking for normal preaching ministry. We met and talked together over a meal in Chinatown. It was great to meet them, but they were equipped way beyond what we had to offer.

What was particularly disappointing was the complete silence on the part of some leaders of large, flourishing churches in London and elsewhere, who failed even to acknowledge our letters asking if they had, or knew of men, who could possibly meet our need. We even wrote to significant men who organized church planting training courses, but received no response; not even to apologise that they knew of no one available currently.

We also had another need at the time. The community in Mayfair had received ten years of visiting, literature distributing, and meetings, with the hope of establishing a gospel church there. With our failure to call an additional leader, there was no way we could delegate a leader to take this work on. Our chief hope was to write to the leaders of a flourishing, inner city London church, asking if it would be possible to designate a small team of mature believers to take the Mayfair group on and grow it for the Lord. Once again, sadly our letter was not even acknowledged. What did happen was that the same church dispatched a hundred of its large congregation to provide the nucleus of a new congregation in Mayfair, based in one of its unused church buildings. Being a strong Bible-based church, all its energy was devoted to a Sunday evening preaching service—with no outreach or identification with the local community!

Taken together, this absence of courtesy and brotherly love was discouraging, and this added to our concerns for the future of the Soho church.

The remaining months passed, but with no eleventh-hour response. By mid-January 2001, the church was ready to recognize Andrew as its lead minister. Pam and I continued to be part of the fellowship on Sunday mornings, but stepped back from the evening programme, to give Andrew space to develop his own ideas.

Memories

A s Christians we are often encouraged to look up or look forward. Hebrews 12:1–3 is an example of this. But some things can only be fully appreciated when life has moved on, and we pause to look back to evaluate the way the Lord has led us. I have done a great deal of this since retiring in 2001. There are dangers in looking back, of course. Few of us have served without fault or failure. Regret, given the opportunity, will eat deeply into us, and rob us of the joy of having served the Lord to the best of our ability, however imperfectly.

Looking back some seventeen years on from retirement, only now can I appreciate that the whole of my previous experience was a preparation for the Soho years. Growing up in the war years, life had few luxuries. We learned to be thankful for what we had. We never stopped to ask ourselves if we were happy, we simply got on with day-to-day living as it was. Our village home was generous in size, but without a bathroom. We washed in the kitchen sink and had to leave the house by the side door and go round to the back to the toilet, without a light. Our clothes were washed on Mondays, by boiling them in a copper in the corner of the scullery. A fire burned underneath to heat the water. Only one room was heated in the winter, the dining room, where the food was also cooked in the black kitchen range which was cleaned with 'Zebo' until it shone. The bedrooms were unheated and, on frosty mornings, ice formed on the inside as well as on the outside of the windows.

We faced danger too, with enemy bombers passing overhead on their night-flights to bomb the London docks twenty-seven miles away. The Battle of Britain was fought in the sky above us and we watched the deadly dog fights, the few defending us against the many. Later, we grew accustomed to 'doodlebugs' belching fire, spitting their way horribly across our skies, chased by RAF Spitfires attempting to tip their wings to direct them away from heavily populated areas, then to explode harmlessly in Kentish fields. When recalling these childhood memories, for me the flat in Marshall Street Dwellings was not the end of the world. Of course, it seemed more primitive to Pam who had moved into a newly built house, with all 'mod-cons,' when she was just three weeks old. She only left it to marry me twenty-two years later.

In a strange way, my lung problems, which began in my pre-school years, played a large part in developing my character: a strong will, an ability to cope with isolation, enforced inactivity, frustration, and disappointment when my closest friends went off to Grammar School, while I had to be content with the local Secondary Modern. This led to a five-year course at Maidstone College of Art, and a National Diploma, the forerunner of the modern BA (hons) degree, having been a schoolboy exhibitor at the Festival of Britain in 1951.

My experience of Christian ministry was never glamorous, and the churches I served were not among the outstanding ones; although the Lord always gave me people and brought many to faith. On two occasions I received enquiries from two large and notable churches looking for a new minister. On each occasion, I was already considering a call to initiate new work: in Thamesmead in 1975, and Soho in 1982. The possibility of preaching to hundreds each Sunday was attractive at one level, yet on both occasions I felt I was better equipped to go to the lost, rather than the found, and to start with no-one, in order to build a church from nothing with the Lord.

The seven years in Thamesmead presented a helpful learning curve, a 'cutting my teeth' experience, in preparation for the really serious task. Surely it wasn't coincidence that most of my commercial experience was based in Central London, and, in the case of the Design Centre, on the very borders of Soho itself. True, there was much to learn about the internal workings of this community, but it was not shocking nor an impossible task. The pieces of my life-puzzle were coming together. This was Romans 8:28 at work.

Of far greater challenge was the prospect of retirement. It would mean laying down everything that filled my heart and hands for some forty years. It would involve parting with the people I cared about and loved deeply. And it would land me with more time than I would know what do with.

With retirement looming, the Rector of St Martin's in the Fields (since appointed Bishop of Salisbury) said to me that for some considerable time I would feel like a tin of rusty nails, rattling around, hardly knowing what was happening to me. If I hadn't been so caught up with all the painting and decorating our retirement bungalow needed, he might have been right.

A special fellowship

I will never forget those Sunday afternoons in Andrew and Joy's home, when Members enjoyed a monthly bring and share lunch, followed by an unhurried Communion Service. We were served the bread and wine, not by deacons but by one another. The home setting seemed so appropriate for such a family occasion.

I also remember those relaxed, Sunday evening fellowship meetings held in Maggi's Mayfair flat. We shared the choice of what we sang, who led the prayers and read the Bible. We usually had a running theme which Andrew or I would introduce. Before we knew it, two hours had passed but not before we had enjoyed delicious home-made cake, and cups of coffee.

Easter, of course, was very meaningful for us, as for all Christians. We felt we had the liberty to use the day in any way that was helpful to us as a city-centre church. We met at Piccadilly at 7 am before making our way down to Waterloo Place, the Duke of York steps, across the Mall, and into St James' Park. We crossed the lake by the bridge dedicated to Diana, Princess of Wales, pausing at its centre to read one of the Gospel accounts of Christ's resurrection, followed by singing a verse of 'Jesus Christ is risen today, Hallelujah!' We walked round the lake, then back to the School in Great Windmill Street. There we shared communion followed by breakfast. With numbers reduced, we held a more informal service, before scattering for the rest of the day.

The work with local young people was always special to me. It was important since city-centre children are so restricted in the size of their homes and absence of gardens. The Boys Own group attempted to make up for what the members lacked in terms of space and male role-models.

A number of boys came from single parent families and had female teachers at Junior School. I was the link between the Play Centre and the Club, while Andrew and Jon provided the strong male active leadership. The Club was disciplined, active, boisterous, noisy—and great fun.

There was a period when we had to get the boys from the Soho School Play Centre to the London City Mission Hall in Covent Garden. The journey involved making our way through busy streets, across the junction of main roads at Cambridge Circus, before heading down narrow streets to our venue. There were always three adults to supervise the journey, but in those days our only 'risk assessment' was to tie the boys together with a length of nylon rope round their arm to keep them together! We needed to watch when passing café tables and chairs on the pavement. Before leaving Soho it was worth checking that chairs, cutlery and sugar bowls had not been hijacked en route. One evening an elderly woman rebuked

The original London City Mission Centre in Covent Garden.
A Sunday service began here in 1987.
The congregation later became an independent church

the leaders for bringing such young lads to a place like Soho, little realizing they all lived there! I will never forget the younger of two brothers who escaped his mother's grasp in Brewer Street and ran into a nearby Sex Club!

Our street literature outreach was a seasonal activity, trying to reach out-of-town visitors to the West End who parked in our patch for several hours in the evening, before driving off again. As a charity we had the right to do this over Christmas and New Year, at Easter, and during the long summer season. We designed and wrote our own literature, always evangelistic, and hopefully catchy enough to encourage inquisitiveness: 'Christmas Presence,' 'Down to Earth,' 'Miracle in a One Star Hotel,' 'Happy Thingummy,' 'Love Found a Way!', 'What if Christmas was only about the office party, a night out with the boys (or girls), or having your mother-in-law to stay on December 25th?'

These titles were followed by a message no longer than two hundred and fifty words. Every tract had the name of the church and a contact number. We were guided by several self-made rules: (1) the weather must be dry, (2) if possible, always give the tract to the driver and (3) never obscure the tax disc. Thousands of these were distributed through the course of the year. Occasionally, there were protests. The editor of the *London Evening News* phoned one morning, possibly having found a tract behind his own windscreen wiper. Could he send a photographer round to get a shot of me doing this work? I went along with the request—and the result was in the next day's edition. The editor thought he recognized my dark red tie with a yellow stripe. Was it a certain Public School tie he wanted to know? 'No, just M&S'.

Most encouraging by far was a telephone call received from a well-spoken woman one Sunday afternoon. She explained she had been cleaning the family car that morning and had found our literature in the glove compartment. She said she had never been to Soho, but added, 'Thank you, it has met my need.'

Improvising

Life and ministry in Soho was never dull. One Wednesday the day was organized for me, with extraordinary

Life and ministry in Soho was never dull

variety. First, it was the day I promised to shave our neighbour, Patrick. It was a 'dressing down' kind of task as everything had to be changed and washed after the job was done. Patrick was up, sort of sober, and sitting in his chair waiting. Yes, the rug was still squelching with urine. Everything went well, and I had the time to have a complete change of clothes before heading off for my second appointment, The National Club, in St James'. I had received an invitation to lead a Bible study for a group of Christian members in the library that morning.

I was surprised to recognize a couple of those present, which helped settle my nerves. A gracious elderly man chaired the study, who explained that he was a deacon at Westminster Chapel. I was immediately struck with guilt that I had spent so little time preparing for this study; I should have given several hours to it earlier in the day, and not depended on my memory of the study of Paul's Letter to the Romans in a series on recent Sunday mornings! I was mortified. The Lord was gracious, knowing the pressure I had been under earlier in the day. The study actually went well, helped by the enthusiastic contributions of several well-taught members. I was invited to stay for lunch—a posh version of sausages and mash!

Through it all, I was conscious that time was rushing by and the Honourable Lady Norton was waiting back in Soho for me to take a Harvest Festival for the group of women she gathered around her once a week. If the morning study lacked preparation, this afternoon Thanksgiving depended on immediate inspiration. Once again, the Lord was gracious, and I was able to dig deep and recall Bible themes and illustrations that seemed to meet the need.

The stress of having to think on my feet was so acute that I was guilty of doing it only once more when, once again, I was under extreme pressure. I had accepted an invitation to speak at the Mid-Sussex Bible Convention in the summer of 2000. The Convention was held at the impressive Bishop Hannington Church, Hove. The morning had been demanding but I left Soho mid-afternoon intending to drive in the hope that I could get home in reasonable time. I had a theme in mind but nothing on paper. Hopefully, the sermon points would sort themselves out in my mind before arriving. The grandeur of the church building immediately daunted me, as did the number of people beginning to arrive. A pianist was playing beautifully on the grand piano. This was evidently a serious occasion. To cap it all, the Conference Secretary announced that the speaker the following month would be Rev Derek Prime, of Charlotte Chapel, Edinburgh. They intended to fly him down for the occasion. All too soon I was introduced and invited to preach. A few days later, the gracious Secretary wrote to thank me for the ministry, commenting, 'It was a time of much blessing ... others have spoken to me about it, and a large number of tapes were sold,' adding, 'We know the praise is really due to the Lord who enabled you.'

Such experience cannot be recommended, but it is probably the price to be paid, at least occasionally, for being available to one's neighbours at all times of the day and night.

Privileges

Without an identifiable building of our own, we seemed to be working out of sight in the shadows of our community. We had nothing outwardly to impress, yet we were noticed and, at times, appreciated. When the Soho Society celebrated its 25th Anniversary I was one of the fifty guests invited to the Reception. Our ex-MP, Lord Brooke, and Simon Jenkins, some-time editor of *The Times*, were there. There were no other clergy or priests to be seen. When our local councillor, Dr David Avery became Lord Mayor of Westminster, Pam and I were among the thirty 'West End' guests invited to the Westminster City Hall for 'drinks.' The view from the tall building was magnificent, overlooking the Palace and its gardens.

Of much greater importance to me was the request made by the Soho Housing Association and a local family, that I be asked to adjudicate in the matter of a fair settlement for damage caused to the home by a blocked drain. There was a fault on the roof which caused rainwater to flood into the tenant's home, spoiling furniture and furnishings. The Association had accepted liability for the faulty drain, but which personal effects had been ruined by the water and which were worn by wear and tear? I did my best to judge the situation without bias, and gave both parties my assessment. The Association accepted my recommendations, but I suspect the family were hoping for a little more.

One of the good things to come out of this 'no-win' situation was a friendship which developed with the staff member who handled this dispute on behalf of the Association. In his early fifties, he was leaving to begin a theological course with a view to being ordained into the Church of England. Since he was likely to end up in one of the liberal seminaries, I invited him home and made him a gift of some of my favourite commentaries.

The four years I spent as a visiting lecturer at the Cornhill Course in the City was a great privilege. The invitation came largely through the recommendation of a friend, Keith Berry, already a student in his second year. Keith had followed the work of London inReach from its inception. In fact he had been considered as a possible leader of the Covent Garden development at one point, but felt his gifting was for preaching and pastoral ministry. Keith felt the Course would benefit from a series of practical lectures which would 'ground' the syllabus based on the Bible, its content, interpretation and application. In 1993 I was invited to join David Jackman, the Director of Studies, for a working lunch in the City. The Cornhill Course was designed for mature students who, for the most part, had achieved their degrees in other fields but who were now seeking to teach the Scriptures in their own churches, or as preparation for full-time ministry.

David was a gracious host, not only providing a sandwich lunch, but a thorough exploration of my conversion, training for the ministry (or the lack of it) ministry in 'normal' churches, and my experience of church planting. He was looking to expose his students to two, one-hour, lectures in one afternoon, following their end of year exams. Would I consider it? Church planting was something I wanted to encourage, and church planters seemed to be thin on the ground. Of course I would take it on. These sessions continued for four years. The first lecture was a survey of what was happening among the churches at the time, and the variety of ways in which they were attempting to plant new churches. The second session was about exposing the situation in Soho: slides, running commentary, followed by comments, lively debate and prayer. I'm not too sure what good I left behind, but I always left the building feeling blessed and encouraged to press on with my work.

Dubious challenges

For entirely different reasons, I remember the morning I decided that my visiting should embrace all and anyone living or working in Soho. Practically, this meant taking a street or block of flats and visiting them systematically. This policy should also include the notorious alleys! Immediately opposite our Brewer Street home, Green's Court linked with Peter's Street. It was narrow and grubby, but tame compared with Walker's Court, which ran parallel to it. An Italian deli, a shoe repair shop, a coffee bar, and a club/brothel were all situated there. The brothel was my first venture into the seedy world of the sex industry.

With a club of sorts trading downstairs, the action seemed to be on the first floor. A highly made-up, bleach-blonde woman in her sixties sat behind a table at the top of the first flight of stairs. I had seen her bustling around the area before. In the 1950s she would have been known as the 'Madame' who sifted the male customers. Apparently, not all male customers were acceptable to the working girls. I explained who I was and why I was visiting all the premises in the Court. She waved me into the waiting room. The room was small and made smaller still by a curtain which separated the waiting customers from those being entertained. The girl was already busy on the other side of the curtain! A few minutes later the customer appeared, embarrassed at finding someone waiting on the other side of the curtain, but he went quickly down the stairs and out into the street.

Then the girl appeared, not wearing a great deal. She was actually attractive, in her early thirties, dark haired, and probably Italian. I explained who I was and why I was there, showing her the family photograph as evidence. She had probably heard many stories like mine before! With customers arriving, time was short. Why was she doing this? I noticed the gold ring on her wedding finger. She said she was working for the money—about £400 a day, lived a train journey away, and was in Soho for about eight hours. Her husband was in agreement with what she was doing. It was time to go. I left some gospel literature behind.

Once again, some would find fault with my visiting such places and people, but Jesus did, and counted such rejects among his friends and followers. I soon recognized that my visiting like this was not ideal, but it was the best we could do at that time.

When preaching away from London one Sunday, I was given hospitality by a single, professional man. When talking openly and frankly after lunch, my host confessed that on occasions he travelled down to Soho to find the sexual experiences he felt he needed. We continued to correspond for some time afterwards, exploring the need of discovering God's will for our lives, and issues about relationships. This incident illustrates the tragic and powerful struggles that can lie behind our apparent respectable churchgoing and loyal Christian service.

Open air witness

Time seemed to be running through my fingers. Easter was a time of year when our congregation was reduced and yet the West End was packed with shoppers. We would plan our Good Friday and Easter Day Services for the few, but I felt we needed to get the message out to the many! But how? It was those young men in their leather jackets and scruffy jeans who gave me the inspiration I needed. They spent hours every day among the crowds with their advertising boards, urging them to make their way to the Beatles' memorabilia shop. If they could do it for the Beatles, why shouldn't I do it for Jesus Christ? Andrew was willing to lead a Service for the few while I tried my hand at some open-air witness.

> We would plan our Good Friday and Easter Day Services for the few, but I felt we needed to get the message out to the many! But how? It was those young men in their leather jackets and scruffy jeans who gave me the inspiration I needed

In good time for Good Friday 1999, I bought an 8′ length of 2″×1″ and a piece of 4′×3′ plywood, which I fixed to the pole. I also knew the message I wanted to share with the shoppers that weekend, and displayed in bold lettering: 1 Corinthians 15:3-4, 'Christ died for our sins according to the Scriptures … he was buried … he was raised on the third day according to the Scriptures.' The crowds began to pour into Piccadilly Circus at 10 am, and I was there to meet them, standing on one of the islands, where thousands would cross with the changing of the lights. Inevitably the gospel brought a variety of responses. A London bus came down Regent Street at speed, its black driver leaning out of his cab, shouting, 'Praise the Lord!' A group of young people from South Africa called out 'God bless you!'

Two men came over and helped themselves to the literature offered. They glanced at it, before screwing it up and deliberately dropping it on the ground. The Japanese family, who by now had become regular members of the congregation, stopped to talk without embarrassment. I was glad when Andrew and Joy arrived with some of the members. They even offered to give me a 'comfort' break in McDonald's, while they held the display for a while. The afternoon was much the same as the morning: large crowds, some looking away, indifferent, a variety of believers stopping to talk, with the occasional abuse, pushing and shoving. I decided to do this again next year, God willing.

Berkeley Square

I'll never forget the delights of study-times spent in the most beautiful of London's Squares—where the nightingales used to sing! In summer, the St James' flat was often impossibly hot, and when the schoolchildren were in the play area it was also impossibly noisy. Laid out in the mid-1700s, and planted with plane trees in 1789, the space and greenery of the Square were a delight. Among the famous who were either born or lived in the surrounding houses, were Horace Walpole, Clive of India, who committed suicide at number 45, Winston Churchill, who lived at number 48 as a child, and Charles Rolls, of 'Rolls Royce' fame who was born here in 1877. Occasionally, my eyes would roam across to the Ladbroke Club where, in 1974, Lord Lucan was last seen before returning to his home and disappearing, leaving behind the body of the family nanny and gambling debts amounting to £250,000. Over the years I spent many productive hours in this beautiful place, without ever hearing a single note of the proverbial nightingale.

No man's debtor

Certainly, the Soho project had been a challenging one, but the hardships, demands and inconveniences weren't a big deal for me. However, none of us live or serve in a vacuum. The decisions we make, the convictions we follow, and the goals we seek, always affect others, not least our nearest and dearest. Soho was a fulfilment for me, but what about Jon, Lois and Pam? Our two eldest, Nick and Jo, may not have been physically involved in the experience but no doubt they often wondered, and worried, about what we were getting into.

Jon mentioned the things he was aware of, and affected by, but he doesn't complain about two of the most serious issues: He was uprooted from a school that he loved for a less than satisfactory school; and his hopes for a graphics course at St Martin's College of Art were dashed by sheer numbers, eighty places and eight hundred applicants. Soho was not the place where you rode your bike round the streets with your friends, or played cricket in the road outside your home. Since he was largely confined to the home, we invested in an Amstrad computer/word processor (PCW) and a range of games popular at the time. The church at Hayes Lane, Bromley, ran a football team which he was able to join. This provided ideal scope for companionship and the sporting activity he needed. With A levels behind him, and a college graphics course out of reach, Jon obtained a junior post with a West End design studio. He progressed to become a senior designer, specializing in video editing and the highly skilled animation process. After some years he, with two colleagues, formed their own company and Jon continues as a self-employed designer today. God is no man's debtor!

For Lois, Soho was, in her words, 'a life-changing' experience. Returning home at weekends she shared her brother's very small box room which doubled as my study. Yet it was in that less than ideal situation that she realised the need to 'trust God and believe in Him and His power'. These are the really important lessons of life, but there were more. Lois writes, 'I also needed to be shown what faith was, and that I could trust Him with my life.' Being the first to believe and be baptized in Soho, Lois soon discovered the implications of being part of a new and fragile church: 'Being in such a small congregation meant that whether you like the limelight or not you must use your gifts. If you don't, the fellowship goes without the helpfulness of your gift.'

When Lois wrote of her experience of Soho, there is no mention of washing in the kitchen sink, the soaking wet wall in the bedroom, or the irritations of sharing a bedroom with a twelve year-old brother. What she does comment on is the fact that God 'does keep his promises … he will never let you down. Keep fighting the fight, and running the race, because the goal is well worth it.' God is no man's debtor!

I'm not too sure now why I didn't ask Pam to give her assessment of these eighteen years. There was certainly no reason to fear a fiery response. Experiencing pangs of guilt following her death in 2010, I asked her sister and a close friend if she had ever expressed her frustration and disgust at the situation in which we found ourselves in the early years—the basement, the toilet with no door, and the kitchen sink doubling up as a wash basin. They both assured me these things may have been recalled in good humour, but never in anger. I was relieved. As the years passed, and the work increased, she grew into a number of essential roles, each of them important to our ministry.

Pam was a sensible, feet-on-the ground woman. She was wise, sensing what was to be done in difficult situations. She was calming with both difficult people and stroppy children. When our children finally left home, Pam was uncomplaining when I was away from home for whole weeks, usually returning in the early hours of the morning. I had been on a week's mission at a church in the north-east. It was at least 3.30 am when I arrived back in Soho and legally parked. I let myself in through the main gate, stairway door, and our front door silently. I undressed in the living room so as not to wake Pam with rustling clothes. My pyjamas were in the bedroom, so I crept along the darkened corridor avoiding the creaky floorboards and slipped into the bedroom. I didn't recognize anything about the room. The bed, wardrobes, chest of drawers, chairs, and everything else, were all in the wrong place. Was I in the wrong apartment? Suddenly a familiar voice broke the silence: 'What time do you call this?' Pam had used the long days alone to rearrange the bedroom!

I suspect Pam's secret was that she maintained a rich and regular time each day with her Lord through guided Bible reading and prayer. This continued until just a few days before she passed peacefully into the presence of her Lord. The theme of that final reading was, 'The promise of heaven is our eternal hope.'

None of the family testimonies contain a hint of outrage, resentment or bitterness. Jon and Lois both wrote having the benefit of hindsight, and so were able to appreciate the blessings that flowed from learning to trust the God who was there, sharing the hardship with them, and turning it to their advantage. Both are where they are today because of the Soho experience. Looking back over these years I suspect Joy would come to the same conclusion.

If the experience seemed comparatively costless to me, I would trace it back to the great revelation of my conversion in 1954. Among the many truths that made an impact on me was that I had been 'redeemed' by Christ. I knew that I was both bought out and brought back by the great price paid by Jesus in his death at Golgotha. The implication was life-changing: neither I, nor my life, was my own but Christ's who paid the redemption price. The apostle Paul says exactly that: 'Do you not know … you are not your own? For you were bought at a price; therefore glorify God' (1 Corinthians 6:19–20). The apostle Peter presses the same point on his readers: 'You were not redeemed with corruptible things, like silver or gold … but with the precious blood of Christ…' (1 Peter 1:18–19).

Given the great price of redemption, it was no great hardship to resign my position at the Design Centre, or to exchange financial security for £8 a week. In serving Christ I found fulfilment and deep joy. Any pain or anxiety came from the implications of my responding to the Lord's call, and its effect on family members. No father could be indifferent to a situation when his children qualified for free school meals, and a uniform grant, or when his son ended up with a second class education, or when it meant a teenage daughter having to use someone else's home from which to leave for her wedding. These give me guilt-pain still. And yes, I would have given a great deal, at the point of retirement after forty years of ministry, to have asked Pam where she would like to live, and, what kind of home would she like to live in, and to have been able to provide it! At the end of the day, all worked out well, and these issues remain a problem only for me.

I am more thankful than I can say that I would not have missed the privilege of working in Soho for the world. The Lord owes me nothing. I owe him everything. For us, the adage became a reality: God is no man's debtor.

To quote from the final *inContact*, there was much to love about the community which was our home but, 'as we go it is the church that we shall miss most of all. Our relationship in Christ has been extraordinarily close and loving. Our love for the Lord, and longing to see him worshipped, honoured and adored has been the catalyst.'

Our new future

It was one thing to promise Pam that retirement would not mean remaining in Central London, but we owned nothing, had no prospect of inheriting anything, and lacked an income to afford a commercial rent. However, through the good services of the Evangelical Housing Association a bungalow in Westgate, in the extreme east of Kent became available. It was in a quiet cul-de-sac, opposite a sizable green. The owners were keen to move and assured us that they would vacate as soon as the sale was complete. Looking at it through displays of plastic flowers, elaborate light fittings, and life-sized glazed leopards, the home seemed basically sound. A timber, L-shaped conservatory, wrapped itself around the front and back of the bungalow, rocking in the breeze.

The Soho church kindly arranged a farewell for us on a Saturday in November 2000. Space, as always, was an issue, but we hired a large room in the Health Centre, Soho Square. Meals were beyond us, but hot and cold drinks, with biscuits would be available. There had been a serious rail crash a few days before just outside London and in consequence all train services were suspended until the entire network had been checked. Would anyone come? In the event, two hundred people managed to arrive somehow, and it was a memorable occasion.

Unknown to Pam and me, the Chairman of the In-reach Project, James Wood, had circulated the supporting churches explaining the financial and accommodation problems we faced when retiring. Caring friends had responded with amazing generosity, and a cheque for £150,000 was presented to us! Some of this amazing gift was used to make up the shortfall on the purchase of the bungalow, and the rest invested to provide income toward the cost of the subsidized rent and Council Tax. This gift made retirement both possible and anxiety free.

Chapter 20

Too soon, our final Sunday morning arrived. It provided one last opportunity to speak to the church and congregation. After the Service we drank coffee, talked informally together, before the final farewells. I walked home, my feet feeling like concrete. Pam would be around for two more days, organizing the removal of our furniture. I was catching a train to Sandwich at 2.30 pm to be near enough to Westgate to pick up the keys of the bungalow in the afternoon. Hopefully, our new home would be clean and ready to receive the furniture when it arrived on Tuesday.

Our new home—déjà vu!

The following day, I had an appointment with a car salesman. The accountant had suggested that transport links in East Kent were a world away from central London and that a car was more of a necessity than a luxury. By the end of the morning, I was the proud owner of a Toyota Yaris. With time to spare before collecting the key to our new home, I checked out the Thanet coast line, shopping facilities and the local churches. I had the distinct feeling that life here was going to be spacious compared with the compact West End.

The arrangement was that I would collect the key to the bungalow from the previous owners at 3 pm. Arriving on time I noticed the removal lorry outside, with the driver sitting in the cab, smoking. I hoped I hadn't kept them waiting. I rang the bell and was quickly ushered into the living room. Nothing was packed or stacked ready for removal. Apparently, there had been a family dispute and the promised muscle power had been withdrawn. The couple were elderly and sitting on the settee having clearly given up! The driver declared that his job was to load and drive the van, not to lift and carry and empty the home; so they had reached stalemate two hours earlier.

At least everyone was agreed that they wanted to get the job done before nightfall. Like an ACAS negotiator I went from the couple to the driver and back until agreement was reached: the driver would stack the furniture in the van, the couple would continue sitting on the settee, while I lugged and dragged their belongings out to the van. Two hours later the empty home was mine, apart from a collection of things the couple felt might be helpful to us. I didn't argue; it would be a simple task to dump later the cardboard boxes, pile of white glazed tiles and the spade with a broken handle.

Pam had remained in Soho, packing up the flat and leaving everything tidy for a homeless Filipino family to move in within days. Paul Mitchell, the director of Herne Bay Court, had kindly offered to provide transport and men to move us to Thanet. I had two days to clear the bungalow of threadbare carpets, plastic flowers and sagging curtains, and clear and clean the kitchen cupboards, scrub the floors and wash down all surfaces. A long-term friend and my daughter Jo were a great help. Pam had begun life in Soho in appalling conditions and I was determined that she wasn't going to arrive to chaos and grime this time.

The bungalow certainly needed redecorating throughout, but we could do that in time. My speciality was emulsion paint on walls and clean lines, while Pam was the expert of non-drip gloss painting. Several areas would need professional help. The timber wrap-around conservatory had broken windows and was decidedly unsteady. It clearly needed replacing. Under the tatty, flea-infested floor coverings, the original Marley tiles may have been all the rage in 1962, but these were now broken and had come adrift from the concrete floor. A gas fire in the living room needed replacing, as did its unattractive 1960s surround. The bathroom and toilet were showing signs of long-term use and little attention, but that would have to wait until the essentials were complete.

For a number of years, I had been booking meetings three years in advance to share the Soho story with churches all over the country. Now, with so much work to be done, I promised to give the first three months to getting the home right before getting involved in travelling and speaking again. Being relieved of so much else, it was relaxing and enjoyable to clean, prepare and paint the entire home, but laying a new laminate floor throughout was a priority. We chose to do it in warm light oak laminate. This done, the redecoration could begin.

One of Pam's longings was to have at least a small garden to tend and grow the plants she had missed for the past eighteen years of flat living. We now had a garden on three sides of the bungalow—all covered in poorly laid crazy paving! To spend money on the garden was a luxury but I felt it was a reasonable outlay in view of the pleasure Pam would derive from it, and my appreciation of her loyalty over the previous forty-six years. My father had died in 1987, leaving me a legacy of £4,000. In view of how much needed to be done, this would not go far, but a local landscaper appreciated our situation and did his best in turning two of the three areas to lawn and building raised beds for planting. Pam would be in her element come the spring.

With £1,500 left in the budget we felt it would be good if we could change the bath, basin and toilet—all stained from years of use. The walls were half-tiled in the same white tiles as the hundreds we planned to dump at the earliest opportunity, but someone had at least made a fair effort to get them straight on the wall. Our new suite may be cheap and plastic but at least we had a clean start. Being without water and the convenience of the bathroom for several days, Paul and Diana Mitchell invited us to stay in a vacant room at Herne Bay Court until all was up and running again. Such loving support did much to heal the pain we felt at leaving the Soho family in those early days.

Our new church family

Next was the need to find a suitable church. Normally, this would have been a key factor in planning for retirement, but we had no choice—it was this bungalow on Kent's north coast or nothing. We had settled our minds on becoming part of a local church if possible since it is a poor witness when travelling out of the area to worship. While engrossed in the painting and decorating we had received visits from two pastors whose churches would have involved travelling out of the area. Within walking distance were four churches: a Catholic, a high Anglican, a United Reformed (with the encouraging sculpture of John Knox on the front of the building) and St James' Anglican church about a mile away. Apart from deciding we needed to worship locally if possible, we also felt we were weary and incapable of meeting the demands another small, struggling church would make of us. Receiving the support of good preaching and a caring fellowship was essential if our retirement was going to be productive in the Lord's work in the long term.

St James' church quickly proved to be the Lord's provision for us. The minister, John Cheeseman, was in the ninth year of his ministry.

With strong preaching and faithful pastoral care he had transformed a small, high Anglican church, into a live, active Reformed evangelical congregation of one hundred and thirty members. Here we were fed, supported by prayer, and encouraged with warm fellowship. We soon began to be refreshed, strengthened and fit for new aspects of service once again.

John and I discovered we had much in common, and quickly became close friends. His biblical view of the church made it possible for me to join the Church Wardens in becoming part of a leadership team. Within five months of our arrival, John was urged by an evangelical bishop to take on the leadership of a large church on the south coast. This was a bitter blow to the local fellowship. The two Church Wardens had a nonconformist background but were drawn to St James' by John's strong preaching. Both men were excellent pastors and leaders of the congregation, but they were not preachers. Faced with a twenty-month interregnum, I was asked to preach on non-communion Sunday mornings, while an excellent retired clergyman was invited to preach each evening. We exchanged duties, morning and evening on first and third Communion Sundays. In the Lord's great goodness, the congregation actually grew numerically during the interregnum period; largely I suspect because we were reaping where John had faithfully sown the precious seed of the Word over the previous ten years!

Eventually, a successor was appointed and normality resumed for the next fifteen years through the ministry of two incumbents. Occasional preaching opportunities were offered at St James' with invitations to preach in a number of other Anglican, Baptist, URC churches and a Seamen's Mission in Ramsgate. One church expected nothing less than a fifty-minute sermon!

One of my commitments was leading a Home Bible Study group inherited from John Cheeseman. The group was originally composed of men and women from St James' but as the years passed it increasingly attracted members from the local URC church, and the neighbours of our hostess in whose home we met. Normally averaging between twelve and fifteen members, the group continued until the month before I left Westgate to settle in Charlwood in 2016.

Chapter 20

Calling time?

Pam eventually encouraged me to 'call time' on at least some of the activities which had gradually dominated our days. In addition to preaching regularly to eight East Kent congregations, I had also been appointed 'evangelist' to St James' church. Now biting into my 70s I was no longer able to cope with the demands of systematic visiting in the parish, but having invested in an Apple Mac computer I still had enthusiasm for writing and producing gospel literature for circulation in the area. A number of teams were formed to distribute what we wanted our neighbours to know about the Saviour and the church, each group concentrating on the homes nearest to where they lived.

Some activities were difficult to lay down. I had been conducting a regular service at a nearby Quaker Care Home for several years on Thursday mornings. Like most of us, I am hoping to face life's end in my own home at the end of the garden in Charlwood, but should professional Care be necessary this Home would be my first choice. There was always a warm welcome. As fragile as the members of the congregation might be, their participation and attention never failed, although the speaker was regularly challenged by one woman who, knowing exactly what she was doing, seemed to take great pleasure in interrupting the flow with loaded questions!

Looking back, I suspect that I wasn't the main reason for the frequent invitations. I can't remember now how it came about, but somehow my dogs got involved and immediately were made welcome. Once my old black and white greyhound girl, Jess, found her way around she would slip out of the meeting room and make her way to the office where she knew the staff would spoil her with biscuits, and she would settle down by the warm radiator. Molly preferred to follow me round the room as I chatted with the congregation before beginning the service. She enjoyed the affection offered but had discovered the bonus of pieces of biscuit being found in the laps of the old folk who had dropped them during their 'elevenses'!

Conducting funerals had also become a regular occupation. Having got to know a local Funeral Director, he regularly passed on the details of families who had no church links but didn't fancy a Humanist funeral for their loved one. Over the course of fifteen years these became cremation services rather than burials, and with it the trend to make the service less 'religious' and more personal. Some of these were very moving military occasions, others were a nightmare due to the behaviour of the 'mourners' and the popular music chosen! Increasingly, families had the freedom to choose the music, style of eulogy and favourite readings, all squeezed into twenty-five minutes. 'Look on the bright side of life' and Frank Sinatra's, 'I did it my way' were the most popular songs sung, and 'If' by Rudyard Kipling the most popular poem. I conducted my last funeral four days before leaving Westgate.

It was an experience in the vestry of a local church which convinced me that Pam was right. It was time to cut back! I was handed an Order of Service just before joining the waiting congregation when I spotted a comment in bold type at the bottom of the final page: 'When the Rev. Toogood was last here his sermon overran, so that there was no time to sing the last hymn. Please be aware of this should it happen again on this occasion.' I felt I didn't need this kind of hassle and decided not to go again if asked. It was now 2009.

Pam's home-call

P am and I began spending more time together, relaxing the schedule which had governed our lives for more than fifty years. With the sea just ten minutes away and the coastal towns of Margate, Broadstairs and Ramsgate all within easy reach, we spent time there. There were pangs of conscience: should we be spending time on ourselves? But with the constant demands of Christian ministry behind us, these became our closest years. We now had time for each other, or so we thought.

The summer of 2010 arrived. Pam had been amazingly well and active through these retirement years but then began to experience bouts of excruciating pain. The GP diagnosed a possible stomach ulcer and prescribed appropriately. When the pain continued a blood test was arranged. Each summer we arranged a house swap with Jon, Jackie and the girls, the youngest of our four families. They loved the seaside, and we certainly enjoyed staying in their village home and taking care of the rabbits and chickens. The GP said it would take time for the results of the blood test to come through, so there was no need to change our plans. The exchange of homes took place on a wet Saturday in the middle of August 2010.

During the first week we had an extraordinary experience. By this time Pam was needing to spend time in bed each afternoon and was still in considerable pain. The following Tuesday we drove into Horley to pick up some medication and returned to find my sister and her husband parked in the drive. I thought we had agreed that they would visit the following week, hoping Pam would be feeling better by then. But it was no problem. We made coffee and began the exchange of family news. Within a few minutes, my brother-in-law indicated we should talk in another room. Richard was a retired senior consultant. He explained he had identified signs that Pam was seriously ill. He advised we left for home that day and insist on seeing the GP that evening. I took them to lunch while Pam slept.

Talking together later, Pam felt we shouldn't spoil the family's enjoyment of Westgate's beaches so soon but wait and see what the coming day would bring. The next morning the decision was taken out of our hands. Our GP phoned to say the results of the blood test were back and that he wanted to see Pam that evening. We phoned the family to let them know we were on our way back, apologizing for spoiling their plans. We arrived mid-afternoon and shared what little information we had. The session with the GP wasn't very enlightening except that he had arranged for a series of scans. The scans taken within a couple of days confirmed that cancer was blocking Pam's bile duct. There was talk of a stent, but nothing was actually done about it.

Scans and interviews continued for the next three weeks which included a nightmare seven-and-a-half-hour round trip to Kings College Hospital in London. This proved to be a waste of time and effort because the latest scan results hadn't arrived! Then we were left on our own. The surgery explained Pam was the hospital's patient, not theirs, and the hospital didn't call until Pam was too ill to get out of bed. Travelling to get another scan was beyond her. That was the last we heard from them!

Pam continued to be in great pain and unable even to sip water. In desperation I went down to the surgery and explained that we needed help. No, I didn't have an appointment. Yes, she was still under the care of the hospital but no-one was doing anything. Thankfully there was a young doctor in the surgery in the process of becoming a partner at the practice. He checked Pam's notes on screen and agreed we needed immediate help. The next morning five nurses turned up at the same time from three different agencies! For the next two weeks we received three visits a day and overnight care on two occasions. We were very thankful. No-one told us that Pam was actually dying and that the help she was receiving was palliative care.

By now, our daughters Jo and Lois had taken leave from their normal work to spend time nursing their Mum. Jon joined us to help with the heavier tasks during this time and Nick called in between his shift-working.

Chapter 21

The Consultant from the Pilgrim Hospice in Margate called to assess the situation. He would speak to us later, but asked to see Pam on her own, his assistant making notes. Joining us a few minutes later, he said he thought Pam would live for a few days. It emerged that she had indicated to him that she wanted nothing that would extend her life by a few days or a week. I shared with him that we had made a pact together on her 70th Birthday. I remembered it well. I had walked the dog at 6 am and was back within the hour. I made tea and took it into the bedroom, with a home-produced card for the occasion. I'd never had a 70-year old wife before, and it seemed to be one of those really significant occasions. The Birthday card was as romantic as I (still only 69!) could make it. Pam had opened it, read it, smiled, and said she thought I must have been thinking of the dog! But then we talked and agreed that if we were ever to become seriously ill we didn't want to be resuscitated. We had both become Christians as students in 1955 and our faith in Christ as Saviour and Lord was still strong. It was far better to be with Christ.

The Consultant explained he was a Catholic and could understand what we had agreed. Pam's pain would be managed and care continued. It was the most helpful visit we had.

Pam died peacefully in the morning of Monday, 4 October 2010.

We were in no hurry to part with her. Jo and Lois washed and dressed her. We each spent time on our own with her, no doubt with our own memories and reasons to be thankful to the Lord for her unfailing love and support. There were tears but we shared a sense of thankfulness that pain was no longer an issue, and that she was with the Lord she loved and served so well.

The GP was informed and came within the hour. His check was momentary, just a touch. The next fifteen minutes were spent sharing his own grief at the death of his father which involved switching off a life support machine, showing that we all are in need of someone to listen and care at such times. The funeral director was expecting our call and arrived mid-morning. Skilfully he kept us talking in the living room while his staff completed their task and drove away without a sound.

Unreality

There was unused medication to pack ready for return to the pharmacy, washing to do and the bedroom to re-arrange. Thankfully the large hospital bed ordered to be delivered had not arrived, which was one problem less to deal with. This done, we felt the need to step back to think through all that still needed to be arranged, and to get a grip on our emotions. It was early October, still warm with sunshine. We walked along the beach, recalling memories and the things to be encouraged by. The coffee shop was welcome. We agreed to

Pam in June 2010, just twelve weeks before her homecall

have lunch—meals had not been the priority over the past two weeks, then the girls must get back to their families. Jon felt he wanted to stay another night; it would have been strange to be alone with only the dog for company.

Inevitably, our 'children' had painful grief to bear and tears were never far away. For me, I was mostly aware of the relief that Pam was out of pain and was with her Saviour, but time was to show that I was living in the unreal world—the unreality that death had removed my life's partner for all time. Reality began to kick in following the Thanksgiving Service eleven days later. Family, friends, and two hundred and fifty supporters shared the service with us. A great sense of warmth and love was felt throughout. Refreshments followed the service, giving opportunity to greet friends from previous churches we had served. Someone said they were surprised that I was able to stand at the door and welcome each guest, but I was still buoyed up by the thankfulness of Pam being without pain and being with her Lord. The human reality still had to kick in.

By 9 o'clock it was time to catch trains or begin the drive home. It was dark and raining hard. Nick dropped me off on his way home. We arrived at the bungalow. I looked out of the car window. It was in darkness, the street light deepening the shadows. Jess, my black and white greyhound was in the kennels until the morning. I put the key in the door and stepped inside to an empty home! A cold was beginning to set in which added to my discomfort. I still hadn't been using the bedroom but a daybed in the study. I suddenly felt isolated, lonely and adrift. It began to dawn on me that I had become a 'widower'. With the sound of rain beating against the window I pulled the duvet from my temporary bed and spent the night on the settee in the living room.

The home was still empty the following morning. I was awake at 5 am and tried to grasp this was the first day of an entirely different kind of life. I was determined to face it and not lean on my family or be a burden to my friends. I made coffee to pass the time, there was still another four hours before I could collect my dog from the kennels.

> I tried to grasp this was the first day of an entirely different kind of life

Perhaps you have been there, this unreal existence that you don't remember from the past, and cannot relate to present experience. Another week passed and a simple service had been planned for the burial of Pam's ashes. It was a Thursday afternoon when the funeral director arrived with a small plastic container. We knew each other well and it should have been a relaxed hand-over, with perhaps a cup of coffee shared. Instead it was tense and difficult. He handed me the container containing about a pound and a half of grey dust and could only manage to say that he would like the container back after the burial, then he was gone. I had been living in the fantasy world of imagining Pam was away visiting family, and that she would be back again in a few days! The ashes placed next to my chair were a solemn reminder of the reality of her loss.

I was engrossed, working on the computer, when I suddenly remembered something that I felt Pam should know. I pushed back the chair, walked out of the study into the living room, and actually opened my mouth to speak. The chair where Pam normally sat, sewing or reading was empty. She wasn't there. Once again, reality kicked in. Very soon 2010 was about to become 2011. Underneath was an old calendar covered in Pam's handwriting. Hair appointments, meetings with friends, grandchildren's birthdays, and much more. Having lived and worked many miles apart for three years after our student days in the 1950s, our relationship was kept alive by regular letter-writing almost every day. The envelope with her handwriting was eagerly sought each day among the rest. Seeing it again caused a rush of sadness.

Lone living raised several other issues. Pam had always handled the money in the family, often making it stretch in difficult times. Pam having been diagnosed and dying within six weeks, I was presented with a steep learning curve. I didn't even know how to get money out of the cash machine. Now I was in charge of working out how much I should spend on the weekly shop for me and Jess, watching how much was needed to cover gas and electricity, rent and Council Tax. Was the car still a necessity or a luxury to do without? Meals were pretty basic from the beginning. They always seemed to involve so much time, buying and preparation, let alone washing up. I eventually slid into slow-cooker meals: chicken pieces, tinned whole tomatoes marinated in hot curry sauce, served with boiled rice. I made it stretch to cover Sunday, Monday, and Wednesday. Kind friends began to invite me to dinner on Tuesdays for a proper meal. Thursdays, Fridays and Saturday's were, 'Whatever's in the fridge' days. This routine continued for the next six years.

Having a dog at home was the greatest single help in recovering normal life. Tess had been a lovely brown brindle girl who was clearly longing to leave the kennels to find a comfortable home. She was a delight and helped us settle into retirement. Sadly, she had to be put to sleep after just five years. Jess had joined us within six months of completing the updating of our home. With enormous fields, once tilled by the monks from the Abbey at Minster, in front of us, and the beach and cliff top walks behind us, a dog was essential. We had already had our daughter's greyhound to stay and enjoyed the experience. Jess, a black and white twenty-two-times winner on the greyhound track at Sittingbourne, took her place. Her racing name was 'Move-along Jewel' because one of her features were tiny white flecks all over the black parts of her body. Almost immediately we received the advice of passers-by who suggested that we take more care when painting the ceiling! As a quality dog, she had continued racing until the age of seven. We gave her a full and happy retirement of a further six years. Molly soon joined her.

I needed to take on a helpful routine, but dog-walking was the only natural ingredient. I was aware of a tendency to be drawn back home every time I ventured into the local shopping centre. For years I had revelled in the opportunity of handling the latest publications in Waterstones. I'm interested in architecture, photography, art, and military history. Combine that with a comfortable chair and a cup of Nero's coffee and I was in another world for an hour or two. But now I felt unsettled, distracted, and aware that for a lone man to sit at a table where couples or a group of young mum's were meeting up for coffee and chat (their children safely in school) was an intrusion. I was usually heading for home within ten minutes, and then wondering why when I put the key into the lock, because there was no-one there; there was no reason to hurry back.

Health issues

Within two months of Pam dying, my skin was beginning to be covered with blisters. Asthmatics usually need treatment for eczema, but this was something not experienced before. Clothes rubbed and chaffed with unpleasant results. Trying to sleep normally became an impossibility. Sitting in an upright chair was the only alternative. Eventually an appointment was made to see my GP who said he didn't know what the problem was. I said I needed help. He said the waiting list at the local Hospital was thirteen weeks. I was willing to pay for help privately. An appointment was made with a Consultant in nearby Canterbury. It was a few days before Christmas.

Following an examination, the Consultant said I was in a shocking state and treatment was urgent. Later he told me he suspected skin cancer was the cause. He prescribed large daily doses of steroids, taken all at once in the morning. There were also lotions for skin care. Soap was not to be used. It was possible to shower, but there was to be no towelling to get dry! I needed to stand and 'air' dry—in mid-December. After three weekly visits, the Consultant said that biopsies were needed and recommended that I become one of his hospital patients. Biopsies cost a great deal and I was his patient for the next two and a half years. The biopsies showed the infection was not cancer but bullous pemphigoid. By all means Google it—but don't look at the images! The infection could have been dismissed as a reaction to bereavement, but it seems to be a genuine disease, not helped by stress. It only affects men and women above the age of sixty-five and takes five years to clear one's system. It is the most degrading and unpleasant of infections. You feel like a leper or like sitting with Job in an ash pit, joining him in scraping yourself with a shard of broken pottery. The condition can kill you if it becomes infected. Recovery is slow.

Approaching my 80th birthday my family and I began to assess my future needs. The cost of living independently was now making inroads into my State pension. My rent was rising, although still well below the commercial level. No one in the family lived close enough to help if I was unwell.

The winter of 2016 was just giving way to spring when I developed a chest infection. The usual steroids and antibiotics were effective to a point but failed to deal with the situation. Easter was approaching and literature had been produced to share its message with the parish. Not wanting to miss out on my favourite roads, I wrapped up against the icy wind blowing off the sea and set out with a large bundle. After an hour and a half I was shivering with the cold and recognized the signs of something more serious developing. I was frustrated that the last long road would not be completed that day but felt I should get home. Once home I still couldn't get warm and began shaking uncontrollably, my head throbbing. I fed the dogs and went to bed and was quickly asleep. During the night I woke to find I was still shivering but had a raging temperature.

I lost track of time but was haunted by the thought that the dogs would need the garden and feeding at some point. Somehow, I made my way across the hall and into the living room to open the door to the garden and propped it open. It was bitterly cold. I could do no more and collapsed back into bed. I slept through the day and another night and woke desperate for a cold drink. At some point I remembered that my daughter Jo was planning to call, I couldn't remember when. She would need to get into the home, so I managed to put the front and inside door on the catch. There was a telephone by the bed but I didn't have the energy or the ability to remember numbers to call for help.

On the third day Jo arrived to find me still with a raging temperature and not able to organize the drink or medication I needed. She phoned the GP, explained the symptoms, and was told to collect steroids and antibiotics in an hour from the local pharmacist. Pneumonia had taken hold. Jo did what she could but had a daughter coming out of hospital later that morning, having given birth to twins and needing help to get home to Tonbridge. At least the dogs and I were set up for the time being.

Once again, the days and nights began to merge. A day or two later a couple of caring friends from St James' realised I hadn't been in touch and wondered if everything was alright. With the doors still unlocked they let themselves in. They immediately took charge and provided the cold drinks I longed for, walked and fed the dogs, and generally provided for what I needed for the day. Over the next few days these kind friends called morning and evening, willing to do anything I needed. After a week I began to feel like eating something, and a small tasty meal was brought each evening. After a week, pleurisy began to develop in my left lung which made it difficult to lie comfortably and kept me awake. I seemed to be going downhill. There was no contact from the GP in spite of knowing that I lived alone. After nine days, Jon reckoned I had had time enough to show that I was improving and realised that I wasn't. In spite of being very busy himself he drove eighty miles from Charlwood to load the dogs and me with a few essentials and drove us to his home. The family dining room was to be my recovery room for the next seven weeks.

As soon as possible I registered with the local Medical Centre in nearby Horley and was fortunate enough to fall into the care of an experienced doctor. It was such a treat to be welcomed with a shake of hands, eye contact when explaining my problems, and no knee-jerk decision to send me to the local hospital for an X-ray. Progress was slow. Several weeks were spent in bed or sitting on a settee for hours every day. The GP stayed on my case and supplied repeat prescriptions when needed.

Only Jon and Jackie had space to accommodate me, even for a short time, but all family members agreed that I ought not to go back to Westgate to continue living independently. A plan gradually unfolded which would allow me to return to my home and dispose of most of its contents while permission was gained to build a Garden Room at the end of Jon and Jackie's long garden, Jon having discovered a company on line which specialized in building these cedar-clad buildings. They were soon on the job. The director travelled down from Cheshire to survey the land available and supplied us with a suggested plan and an estimate of the costs involved. There were challenges, and the local authority imposed certain conditions. The plans were exciting. The building would have lots of glass to make the most of the fields and great oak trees at the back. Work could begin in June and be complete and ready for occupation within six weeks.

One great sadness occurred just before returning. Still sleeping in the dining room, I was aware of noises coming from the living room next door. More than once I concluded it was the dogs either re-making their beds or swapping them as they often did during the night. Eventually, when going to check, I discovered that it was Jess, struggling to get to the water bowl but crashing down again, her hind quarters having given way. At the age of thirteen she had reached the end of her natural life and it would be kind to put her to sleep that day. The vet made an appointment for this to be done at 6 pm that evening. There was no protest, she simply went to sleep.

Once more I came back to the empty home, now looking neglected since I left it in emergency almost two months before. It was strange not having Jess. Her empty bed was in the corner by the fireplace. Molly was confused by it all and immediately occupied the vacant bed.

I busied myself packing what I needed to take and saying farewell to many good friends. I was keen to recycle whatever I did not need and was assured that a certain well-known charity could be relied upon to help. The men arrived and went from room to room passing judgement on various items: yes to the fridge and washing machine but no to the computer desk and conservatory furniture. Seeing that I would be lumbered with items that could not be recycled, I said there would be no cherry-picking— take the lot or nothing! They were not impressed, made an unpleasant comment and left the home, noisily closing the front door. Apparently 'charity' had become a hard-nosed business operation.

The experience left me stunned for a day or too but then Jo noticed a charity shop in the high street which raised funds to support those who cared for family members. Yes, of course they would come and see what I had. They were simply wonderful, and not only took the things rejected by the other charity but also things I had put on one side to unload at the dump. They called twice while I was in the process of sorting and packing, and again when my family was loading the van the day after I had moved out. They deserved to prosper.

Molly didn't enjoy seeing the home being disrupted and took refuge in her bed, reluctant to leave it for a walk or even to get her food. She was clearly missing Jess. After a week, I drove to the re-homing kennels. Did they have a girl who would live happily with brindle Molly? The staff had other ideas. For six months they had been nursing a blue brindle boy back to health. He had been neglected with his female partner in someone's back garden. Not only were the dogs exposed to all weathers but had been starved of food. The girl looked as if she may not survive. The boy was sweet natured, a rare blue brindle, and desperate to find a loving home. He was brought out to meet us, and Molly seemed quite at home with him. I walked the dogs through country lanes, Molly was happy with the arrangement, so long as she was in the lead. The new boy, Merlin, was at the back!

Several neighbours came to say goodbye before work on my last morning. I began to feel the pressure and felt the need to close the door and begin the journey to Surrey. I left a note to the family arriving the following day, apologizing that with energy and space used up, I had left more for them to do than I hoped. I drove away earlier than planned at 9.30 am on 31 May 2016. I didn't look back. The rain was torrential. A new adventure was about to begin.

Another new home and church

A rriving in Charlwood, Merlin was immediately fussed and fondled and made to feel welcome. He revelled in the attention and settled immediately into the family.

Delayed by a week, two Swift builders arrived on the doorstep at 8 am on Monday 13 June 2016. Lee and Steve proved to be multi-skilled, hardworking and reliable men. They worked twelve hours a day, five days a week during the wettest June on record. Having failed to get permission to bring a small digger down a neighbouring field, the foundations of the Garden Room had to be dug by hand. In the following days the building arrived in large ready-made parts, accurate to the millimetre. With no other access to the site available, everything had to come through the family home: wheelbarrow loads of soil, ready-built sections of the building and heavy tools. Jackie was very patient with the muddy boots that passed through her hall, kitchen and living room many times a day. Each day ended with a big clean-up. Four weeks later, I was moving all my belongings into my new home. Health issues persisted and I seemed to be picking up infections on a regular basis. Someone had warned me that getting clear of pneumonia normally takes two years!

The village of Charlwood had once offered a variety of places of worship but only the parish church survived the years. The building had Saxon foundations with a Norman main structure which was added within fourteen years of the Norman invasion. A large extension was built in 1284 by a wealthy local family in the hope that this would aid a family member through the fiery experience of purgatory!

The parish church was a gentle five-minute walk from my home. If it was important to worship locally in Westgate it was certainly more important here. The church might be described as 'traditional' and the services followed the Book of Common Prayer. I began by attending the 8 am communion service. Not surprisingly it was totally different from what I had been used to, yet just what I needed at this point in my recovery. Numbers attending varied between eight and ten. We sat in the choir stalls and responded to the prayers and the Creed. There were no hymns. The silence and reverence were very helpful. The reading of the epistle and gospel (read as we stood) was followed by a comment drawn from the Gospel. Solemn words prepared us to receive the elements of bread and wine. Following the final prayer, the congregation sat silently until the celebrant had returned to the vestry, the sign for the congregation to leave quietly. The service had lasted forty minutes, which was as much as I could take at that point. This pattern continued for the next eight months.

As health returned, I realised I would need to attend the 9.30 am service if I was to become part of this worshipping community. An impressive peal of six bells began at 9 am and continued until the choir and clergy filed into the worship area. Each Sunday of the month had its own shape but all Cranmer in origin. For a village church, it was well supported and organized, a surprising number of people welcoming, reading, praying and assisting the priest-in-charge in serving communion. A choir, accompanied by an accomplished organist, led the congregational singing well. A choir of young children (Larks and Linnets) contributed delightfully to the monthly family service. The preaching was brief but found its theme in the Bible readings designated for that day. Coffee followed the hour-long service.

For several months I was content to sit quietly toward the back of the congregation, receiving what helped and strengthened me. I sensed there were things I wasn't up to doing but felt increasingly that there was a ministry of gospel literature which I could fulfil. Congregations swelled encouragingly at certain times of the year: Remembrance Sunday and, of course, Christmas and Easter. In my second year as a member of the congregation I invested in one hundred and fifty copies of a booklet produced by Lifewords and sought permission from the clergy team to distribute these at Easter. Believing that a church's notice-board is its shop window I regularly produced posters with a gospel message fitting the occasion. During the next year I declined an invitation to become a member of the PCC. The very thought of long evening meetings, with debate, disagreement and especially endless financial reports was still beyond me.

I began service in small ways but was especially pleased to contribute to church life when invited to lead a drop-in prayer group on Thursday mornings. Numerical growth was slow but so encouraging in terms of increasing warmth and fellowship—and the fascination of heading up something no one could ever recall having been done before. Time was given to discovering the prayer life of the Early Church in Acts which taught us much about its priority, fervour and commitment. With Easter approaching we used five weeks to cover the themes of the Upper Room, Gethsemane, the Trials of Jesus, the Crucifixion and Resurrection. Having completed these themes the group agreed that we should be spending valuable time in Bible study as well as prayer. As I write, we have begun to read and discuss J C Ryle's small booklet, 'Do You Pray?' Later I want to introduce the book of 'Ruth' in the hope of showing that Bible study doesn't need to be 'heavy' or 'dull' but warm, thrilling, and full of good news.

Providence Chapel

Two hundred years earlier, a local farmer had heard of a timber guardroom that was for sale in Horsham. It had been built when there was a possibility that Napoleon might invade, but after Waterloo the building was offered for sale. The farmer bought it, loaded it onto horse-drawn wagons and transported it to Charlwood where, in 1816, it was rebuilt as a place of nonconformist worship. Over many years Providence Chapel attracted families from surrounding villages to its morning and afternoon services and Sunday School. At one point the size of its congregation equalled that of the parish church, but it dwindled until the last member died in 2013. The building was closed. In need of major renovation, Providence Chapel was sold and new Trustees were appointed. Extensive repairs took place over the next two years, funded by the Lottery Fund.

Two or three years before my arrival in Charlwood, an attempt had been made by Maidenbower Baptist Church, Crawley, to plant a church in the village, based in the parish hall. Regular visiting had been undertaken, a stall taken at the annual fête, and the possibility of buying or renting a home in Charlwood seriously considered. One or two locals dropped into the Sunday afternoon service over the three-year period but none settled. Eventually the church felt it should draw back and cover the project with prayer.

To their credit, the Trustees of the old Providence Chapel, conscious of the many years the building had served as a place of Christian worship, invited nonconformist churches in the area to hold a service of thanksgiving for the past, and a re-dedication of the building to its new purpose of providing additional space for the village school and a meeting place for community meetings. Provision was also made for the Chapel to be used for occasional Christian worship.

A Service of Rededication was held on 3 February 2019 which I had the privilege of leading, when a hundred people with links to the old Chapel came together. It was standing room only. The singing was amazing, the fellowship warm, and the preaching challenging. The pastor of Maidenbower Baptist Church, Crawley, plans to begin a monthly meeting on the first Sunday afternoon of each month, based in the Chapel. Who knows where that could lead?

A disastrous encounter!

It is almost three years since I arrived in the village. Life has been quite an adventure, but these most recent years have brought a variety of trials and not a few tears. More than once I thought I must have taken a wrong turning at one point or another, and more than once I would have given a great deal to have been somewhere else. Probably most of us could say the same when looking back over long lives.

For many years I have found it helpful to make a record of life's varied experiences. As believers in the Lord Jesus, we know we have his presence and gracious guiding at every point of our lives. We therefore expect there to be a purpose in each path we take. It is not only that he knows the path we take, but that he directs our path as we follow him. Divine providence is a wonderful reality, although usually only appreciated when we look back over many years.

It was a particularly serious bout of pneumonia which brought me to Charlwood initially, and with airways already narrowed or closed because of untreated chronic asthma as a child, chest infections, pleurisy and heavy colds were regular occurrences, especially during the winter.

This situation wasn't helped at all by an incident which almost brought me to total despair within three months of arriving in the village. It was a lovely day and the dogs were enjoying their freedom. I was bending down to clip the lead onto Merlin's collar when he suddenly broke free and raced away in the direction of the houses nearby, closely followed by Molly. Suspecting it was a cat that had caught their eye, I hurried after them as quickly as I could. Too late, Merlin had caught the cat and was shaking it. I grabbed him firmly and he put the cat down. The owners were understandably distraught. Strong language and anger flowed. Neighbours gathered to see what the noise was all about. The atmosphere was very tense. My attempts to apologize, and to help in any way I could was brought to an abrupt end and I was ordered off the bereaved owner's property. I was told the police would be called. I thought it best to go home and await whoever was going to investigate the incident. The dogs were subdued.

I was absolutely distraught. My one ambition in coming to live in the village was to live a quiet life and to be a clear witness for Jesus Christ. A single incident and this disappeared. I woke the next morning hoping it had all be a terrible dream. I was trapped. My old home had been sold within a week of my leaving it. I had signed papers agreeing to re-home the greyhounds, and not to breed from them, or to race them, or keep them out in the garden, but to care for them for the rest of their natural lives. They could not be returned to the kennels. To make matters worse, Jon and Jackie were on holiday in France and wouldn't be back for another ten days.

Later that day the Borough's Animal Warden arrived on the doorstep. The police were not concerned about the incident, but he had been given the task to sort it. He had already seen the cat's owners and told me how angry and upset they were. As an ex-military policeman he exuded authority and performed his task with due formality. I told him exactly what had happened, which he appreciated; offending dog owners

Michael's two greyhounds in 2019, Molly (front) and Merlin

apparently rarely if ever accept that their pet was at fault. Talking together we discovered we were both Christians. What could I do to help? I asked. A vet had been called the previous day and had confirmed the cat was dead. The couple said they were expecting me to pay the vet's fee and also the cost of having the cat cremated. I agreed to pay the £223; but they didn't want to meet me. The warden had reported the incident to the Local Authority which required me to muzzle the dogs whenever I walked them through the village.

This regrettable incident was to have wider implications than I imagined. I had written two sample articles for the parish magazine which circulated throughout the village. I thought it lacked a positive Christian message and so was attempting to remedy this. What could be objectionable about themes based on Lord's Prayer? The following Sunday I received a call from the editor explaining that the incident involving the cat had been discussed after the 9.30 am service. Not only were the cat's owners regular members of the congregation but the man was a member of the choir. He had made it known that should he see me at any of the church services then he would leave immediately. The editor said it would not be appropriate to include my articles in the present circumstances so would not be using them. Discussing the situation with the minister, it was agreed that I could continue to attend the 8 am service but no other until the situation had been resolved. I was covered in shame and undoubtedly the talk of the whole village. I could only pray.

Eight months later something wonderful happened. A phone call from the assistant minister invited me to meet him, the offended couple and a church warden, in the church vestry the following Wednesday afternoon. We each had an opportunity to share our part in the sad experience, and on my part, to offer a sincere apology for what had happened. To my surprise the owner of the cat said he also needed to apologize to me for his anger displayed and the language he used on the day in question. Two hours later, we shook hands and the minister closed the meeting in prayer.

There are better and easier ways of forging friendships but that is what happened that afternoon. The following week I was invited to the home for coffee, and the following week also. Over the past two years we have been out for lunch and usually make sure we talk together over coffee following the 9.30 am service on Sundays. We also kneel together at the Communion rail and receive the bread and wine, symbols of Christ's body and blood given for us. Looking back on my first year in Charlwood I was inclined to think that the cat encounter was enough of a trial for the entire twelve months I had been here, but there was more.

Chapter 22

Burnout

In moving home from Westgate I had left behind all my previous responsibilities. It was a clean start, a new beginning, and yet I suffered an experience which is now generally identified as 'burnout.' Why the condition showed itself was a mystery. I was living in the loveliest home I had known in more than fifty years. It was equipped with everything a lone man and his two dogs needed. Set in beautiful countryside, it overlooked green fields, great oak trees and four hundred-year-old cottages. The wildlife was a delight. I had a loving family thirty yards away with whom I shared a meal every evening. I had two lovely retired greyhounds to keep me company. Despite all this, a totally destructive experience of burnout took hold and reduced me to a heap of dust for several months.

It was then that I discovered Christopher Ash's excellent book, *Zeal without Burnout*. Christopher was writing from personal experience having recently emerged from the condition. There were differences between our respective conditions. His was primarily a spiritual experience (an overload of research, study and lecturing) while mine was essentially physical (long courses of strong medication treating serious illnesses, plus several experiences which undermined my general health, reserves and confidence). A different cause perhaps, but the effects were identical:

> The complete loss of energy, drive, initiative and desire.
> An open Bible, but without the ability to read, work, or write.
> Letters unopened and emails left unanswered.
> Prayer requests, but without the strength to pray for myself let alone others.

My experiences were identical but there was another challenge:

> The sheer horror of the telephone ringing and there being no-one else to answer it or to deal with the request made.

Christopher Ash summarized the condition of the burnout victim: 'He has nothing left, no resources, no emotional reserves, no intellectual energy, nothing.'

I particularly appreciated Christopher's 'Acknowledgements' where he suggests the clue for his own complete recovery: 'My deepest human debt is to my wife, Carolyn, who walked through all these experiences with me, with consistent patient love and wisdom. He who finds such a wife finds a very great blessing.'

Although I felt that anything I had done or been in the past accounted for absolutely nothing, I sensed that in some way the experience originated with the Lord to humble me afresh and bring me to his feet. Others said I should have been more aware of Satan who may also be playing a part in the whole experience, if not all of it.

> I sensed that in some way the experience originated with the Lord to humble me afresh and bring me to his feet

Some damaging aspects of burnout could be permanent. It was well over a year later that I was asked to take a Bible reading at the crowded parish Candlelight Service. I discovered that though I had spent fifty-five years as a minister, full-time and in retirement, the thought of stepping up to read the Bible publicly put me under the most severe stress both before and after the event. I still feel uneasy about leading the prayers or serving communion. I am frustrated by no longer being able to sing or read with a strong, clear voice. Now and again, I am invited to special occasions when there is a point when I feel that energy is draining away, and I have to ask to be excused and hurry home. Long telephone conversations and over-staying visitors exhaust me still—two years after the experience.

I am sharing aspects of the eventful first 365 days of my life in Charlwood, but there was much more. For example, the family dog was crushed and eventually died when I encountered a non-stop driver on a narrow, one-way street in the village ... and another when my car, parked overnight in the same one-way street, was battered by a driver who had evidently been drinking and driving ... or the dark early morning, while leading my dogs through the village en-route for the Glebe, when a cat ran out of the hedge under their noses and they gave chase. The traffic was speeding through the narrow street, so to have let the dogs go would have been instant death. Being dragged forward I was on the point of falling, when I crashed into a signpost pointing the way to the 11th century church. The impact was down my left side, leaving me winded. Thankfully I was wearing my fleece-lined, dry-as-a-bone winter coat, which must have saved some broken ribs. The incident set off another bout of pleurisy which kept me sitting up in bed at night for the next five weeks.

Hope never disappoints

The string of damaging experiences during the first twelve months in Charlwood were extraordinary. I had known nothing like it in the previous sixty years. There were so many experiences, coming so closely together, that they could hardly have been coincidental. I sensed the Lord was involved, probably with some disciplinary purpose in mind. But what was I lacking? Faith? Trust? Obedience? Or was I proud and arrogant and in need of humbling?

In the darkest days, I wondered momentarily, if I had not experienced enough fiery trials in the course of more than forty years of Christian service for Jesus. Hadn't my pastoral and church planting ministry been costly enough? Hadn't we, as a family, had to look to the Lord for our financial needs over many years? Wasn't it testing enough to live among the lowest of the low in that basement flat? And how humbling to reach retirement and not be able to afford the rent of a basic home. Having already been bereaved of a much-loved wife, and laid low with pneumonia and a variety of other serious lung conditions, hadn't I been hammered enough? I was, like Job, reduced to a pile of ashes.

> How humbling to reach retirement and not be able to afford the rent of a basic home

In his letter to the Christians in Rome, the apostle Paul draws together the most curious and contradictory of experiences within the scope of just five verses in chapter five. He begins with the good news that 'We have been justified through faith', and that we have 'peace with God through our Lord Jesus Christ.' He tops it all by pointing out that, 'through faith, we have gained access into this grace in which we now stand.' Marvellous! Our response is to 'rejoice in the hope of the glory of God.' There is no problem there! But now the apostle suggests that we are to 'rejoice in our sufferings.' How does that work? The apostle's 'Because' explains how. Suffering, rightly understood, is a bonus—it teaches us to persevere, and not give up. And perseverance is an asset because it produces character, it toughens us up. Character is good because it produces hope, that is, confident expectation. And hope never fails or disappoints.

Everything has changed in Mayfair now, but a few years ago there was a bronze sculpture where New and Old Bond Street met. The sculpture figured reeds with mallard ducks in flight; in fact it was a fountain. The water emerged from the top of the design and flowed down through a series of cups which, when full, overflowed to fill another cup further down— just as suffering flows into perseverance, perseverance into character, and character into hope, which is confident expectation. Hope is worth everything. It never fails or disappoints.

I recently had an appointment with the consultant who regularly scans and checks the condition of my lungs. He had just received a report following a PET scan at the Royal Marsden Hospital. A cancer had been diagnosed in my left lung. So, another adventure beckons and another trial of faith appears on the horizon. But there is no reason to be afraid because, as the apostle says, 'Hope does not disappoint us, because God has poured out his love into our hearts by the Holy Spirit whom he has given us.'